APPLAUSE FOR

COMPLEXPEOPLE

COMPLEXPEOPLE

[Insights at the Intersection of
Black Culture and American Social Life]

DARYL C. HOWARD, PH.D.

Complex People: Insights at the Intersection of Black Culture and American Social Life

Published by
HUE Initiatives Press
P.O. Box 1591
Laurel, MD 20707
www.hueinitiatives.org

Cover/Interior Design and Portrait by Mareta Creations (www.maretacreations.com)

To my ancestors of the past…
To the beautiful present…
To the future of my children's children.

ACKNOWLEDGMENTS

No book is done in isolation. I have many people to whom I need to express gratitude.

First, a big shout-out to my students and colleagues who support, compliment, and challenge my pedagogy. You make me constantly reflect on my work and aspire to become a better thinker and educator.

To Makya Renée Taylor of Mareta Creations, thank you for processing my ideas about this project. Taking a concept and making it into art is not an easy task. I thank you for your attention to detail.

I am grateful for CeCe Whittaker and Rebecca Fowler's editorial support. CeCe, you saw things that were not evident to me at first glance, and Rebecca, your edits, ideas, and dedicated support in the final stretch were a definite blessing. Thank you.

Words of appreciation are also extended to Bernadette Connor. This book was stubborn and you were there to advise and encourage during uncertain times.

To the achievers, my brothers of Kappa Alpha Psi Fraternity, Incorporated, Kappa Gamma Chapter: Thank you for the bond we share that pushes us to achieve in every field of human endeavor.

I would be remiss if I did not mention the HUE Initiatives nonprofit team as well as our book club and online discussion group. In particular, Ryan Stinson and Kenny Smith receive kudos for listening to my endless excitement (and frustration) about this project. Unfortunately, there are too many others in the circle to name but it has been the group's agitation, support, and desire for social change that has challenged me to think and produce.

My family is the best. All of them. In specific, I am forever indebted to my parents, Billy and Barbara Howard, for every prayer and provision. These blessings have not been overlooked.

To my children, Cambel, Cori, and Daril Naomi. You have taught me a lot about myself. The love, laughs, and lessons are constant and I strive to be a great dad because of you.

Beside every good man, stands a good woman. Consistency and support are essential in this world we live in. To my beautiful wife, Michelle, I appreciate your love and partnership. I love you.

Lastly, this work would have never been completed without the blessing of the Creator.

Thank you, God.

TABLE OF CONTENTS

PREFACE

Due to its complexity, race is not an easy topic for Americans to engage. However, when placed in context, racial images, ideas, and issues are given shape. My intention in writing *Complex People* is to help give shape to aspects of black American culture as it relates to systemic, yet fluid, American constructs. This book has been written in the Obama era, which, arguably, started with great optimism for improved race relations and efforts toward social equality. However, based on the last few years, this era now leaves us with more questions to those dynamics than we have answers.

In this ever-evolving society, I understand clearly that one body of work cannot fully address all of the issues. Accepting those limitations, I sense it is now time to move on from this project and advance into a new space where I can expand on these, as well as new, ideas. As for *Complex People*, the goal has never been about confirming or refuting stereotypes or proposing immediate solutions to our problems. This book is purely about helping the reader to recognize what I believe to be a simple truth — that all people deserve to be fully contextualized in order to understand and, most importantly, appreciate their humanity.

Queens proud underestimated STRONG
ORANT undervalued RESILIENT Violent Marginalized CREATIVE Lazy
ritual Dependent OPPRESSED Smart Confused Free athletic
ponsible LOUD Articulate THUG Brilliant inferior KING
ovative Artistic REGAL Queens Broken underestir
TRONG IGNORANT undervalued RESILIENT Violent Ma
ATIVE Lazy Conditioned Spiritual Dependent OPPRESSED Smart o
letic Stupid Irresponsible LOUD Articulate THUG Brillia
NGS slaves Innovative Artistic REGAL Queens Broke
derestimated STRONG IGNORANT undervalued
lent Marginalized CREATIVE Lazy Conditioned Spiritual Dependent
art Confused Free athletic Stupid Irresponsible LOUD A
IUG Brilliant inferior KINGS slaves Innovative Artistic REG
Queens Broken underestimated STRO
ORANT undervalued RESILIENT Violent Marginalized CREATIVE Lazy
ritual Dependent OPPRESSED Smart Confused Free athletic

INTRODUCTION

[WHY THIS MATTERS]

I've always wanted to complete a project that made a contribution to my culture. Due to my curiosity and unyielding passion for these topics, I know that these observations have value. I've always been one who has thought deeply about the world, both the beauty and horror of it, and what would be my ultimate offering to it. Through my education, teaching, and organizing, I believe I have been able to make a small imprint. The focus of my mission has been to raise the consciousness of my fellow citizens, particularly young people, mostly of color, all with the goal of creating a more human-centered society. This ideal society, as I envision it, is not some type of utopia, but, similar to the South African concept of *ubuntu*, simply a place where there is an ever-present understanding that human beings need other human beings.

My personal journey to this awareness has occurred over many years. It's funny how one can look back over time and see significant development in ideas and personal philosophy. This development includes the influence of family, friends,

1

education, and efforts toward social change, as well as technological advancements, world events, etc., all of which have contributed to my growth. At my age, I feel pretty firm in my ideological location and that I can live in peace in this space for some time. My journey has been an enjoyable one and I hope that my writing, teaching, and any efforts toward exposing the beauty of higher intellectual exercise will be useful.

Within this work, I've tried to humanize my thoughts, meaning that I have attempted to take some abstract notions in my mind and give them life through personal experience and other relevant examples. To some, this text will be considered new material, while to others it may be just a varied replication of the many assumptions that already exist in society. Based on the aforementioned statement, if there were an ideal audience for this work, I would envision that young adults would find the most value in the content herein. I've had awesome experiences in the classroom and in front of various high school and college-aged audiences so I chose to write the essays in that same engaging style. Although the delivery comes across as personal, the insights are quite academic. I've written with a concise and common sense approach that exposes new ideas and challenges to the current thinking, yet is not so cumbersome that the reader would become fatigued and thereby disengage from the conversation.

I would like to think that my doctoral studies and dissertation, an analysis of sociocultural philosophies, played a part in my wanting to share these ideas with the world. First, having to travel abroad to complete my research and observing other cultures in action helped me to understand how the world is so much bigger than the communities where we grew up or presently reside. Challenged to recognize customs and traditions that were foreign to me, I embarked on a new leg of my identity-forming process. I am not me without those experiences. I also attribute my exposure over time, in person and print, to some incredible thinkers. They have created within me a desire to be another vessel in the sharing of old and new ideas with those whom I encounter.

As a conduit of cultural ideas, this work shares many of my lessons I have learned and lectures I have delivered over the years. Returning to my academic roots of Sociology, and now teaching in the discipline, I can see the theories I was exposed to years ago having blossomed from a newly planted tree to a mighty oak. Some of my lectures, in their original versions, appear fragile and vague in comparison to the current editions of the same topics. Even now, it is a scary thought to imagine how shallow this text may look to me in a few years. As a support, I use many sociological sources, quotes, and concepts in this work to guide and reinforce where my current thinking exists. These are also helpful in highlighting academic boundaries to respect or debunk and to expose certain notions as legitimate or irrelevant.

For the sake of my own sanity, I take pride in seeing this book simply as an ever-developing work of art. In order to consider oneself a thinker, one must routinely, through writing, unleash thoughts and ideas to allow for new ones. This shouldn't be a surprise due to the nature of the topics that I am engaging. This work examines many of the institutions of American society, such as education, politics, media, and the family, and places them in context with issues of racial and gender inequality. Every essay in this work speaks to the processes and patterns of these entities and how they have been established, maintained, or changed over a period of years. I chose the title of the text with this in mind, as each of these societal dynamics has complex and nuanced meanings based on whom one asks. Operating from a black American lens, I thought it critical for the world to hear from that particular cultural context.

More specifically, *Complex People* is a work that brings our subconscious understandings and positions on race, gender, and other societal dynamics to light.

This book's analysis of black culture and American social life can be described as complex from two different angles. First, when individuals are misunderstood or wronged, their behavioral response may be tainted as it relates to that issue or experience. Some may say that this person has developed a *complex*. Black Americans have certainly lived with this dispersion having an identity that's been born and formed under duress. It will take more than calls to "get over it," to reconcile this complex and the feelings of resentment for helping build a country yet never being recognized as a contributor. Furthermore, on a larger scale, all American citizens are *complex*. We are indeed an interesting country because we collectively profess that we want freedom, opportunity, and equality for all. However, due to known and unknown biases, we struggle to make the cultural calculations of how these things mean different things to different people. Due to its complex history and conflicting definitions of these ideals, America has yet to fully crystallize the cooperative and free society that it touts.

Writing with that backdrop in mind, I believe that all curious and open-minded learners will find these essays filled with unique insights. These observations can be consumed in any order. They are interdependent as social issues but not dependent on one another as if in an attempt to maintain a storyline. My simple goal is to prod and challenge the reader to deal with the realities discussed within this work. I want to educate readers to the idea that the minority perspective should be sought and valued, as this is indeed one part of a larger, mainstream picture. It would seem that most would embrace that sentiment. However, the quest for, or maintenance of, power often destroys attempts toward collective understanding and seeks to highlight differences for which to make deficits. Opposed to examinations of meaningless qualifiers, pluralism can and will thrive when the beauty of all culture is explored and respected.

I hope this text will allow the reader to appreciate the intricacy of cultural contexts as they are of critical importance in a pluralistic society. Again, we process society's institutions and inequality through our individual contextual lens. This is exactly why we begin many statements with "In my opinion" or "From my experience," and most of us lack the empathy or sociological imagination to see something any other way than our own. Social awareness is essential as the unwritten rules of society can have consequences that are either rewarding or tragic. A high degree of social competency should be our goal, if not for the maintenance of the larger society, then at least for the sake of our own personal growth. It is my aim within this book to make some sense of these matters, particularly for those who desire to scratch the surface in understanding aspects of black American cultural and contextual identity. I hope I can do this assertion justice.

Queens **STRO** underestimated **STRO**

ORANT undervalued RESILIENT Violent Marginalized CREATIVE Lazy

ritual Dependent OPPRESSED Smart Confused Free athletic

ponsible **LOUD** Articulate THUG Brilliant inferior KINGS

ovative Artistic REGAL Queens **Broken** underestir

TRONG IGNORANT undervalued RESILIENT Violent Ma

ATIVE Lazy Conditioned Spiritual Dependent OPPRESSED Smart c

letic Stupid Irresponsible **LOUD** Articulate THUG Brillia

NGS slaves Innovative Artistic REGAL Queens **Broke**

derestimated **STRONG** IGNORANT undervalued

lent Marginalized CREATIVE Lazy Conditioned Spiritual Dependent

rt Confused Free athletic Stupid Irresponsible **LOUD** A

IUG Brilliant inferior KINGS slaves Innovative Artistic REG

Queens **Broken** underestimated **STRO**

ORANT undervalued RESILIENT Violent Marginalized CREATIVE Lazy

ritual Dependent OPPRESSED Smart Confused Free athletic

CREATE YOUR VALUE

[AMERICAN EDUCATION AND SOCIAL AWARENESS]

In any society, the presence of educated and aware citizens is imperative. More specifically, for any society to flourish, or at least maintain itself, there has to be a continuous regeneration of ideas and influences that encourage growth and development. From the tangible to the intangible, or reverse, the transmission of culture must take place. In fact, nations are placed on a spectrum perceivably as "super-power" or "developing" solely because of the sound or faulty construction and maintenance of that society.

This essay examines the value of education and awareness in American society. Using the text, *Social Problems and the Quality of Life* to initiate a template for thought, I reflect on the functions of education in three ways: creating good and effective citizens, providing individuals with the possibility of upward mobility, and liberating people from the bonds of ignorance (Lauer and Lauer 2013). I would like to further simplify these classifications into new categories such as the maintenance of culture and society, the pursuit of cash and status,

9

and, lastly, individual growth and personal success. Education, or the inter-generational transformation of knowledge, is best examined through these categories in order to view the full and cumulative scope of its importance.

CULTURE AND SOCIETY

Examination of these ideas requires that we begin by thinking of all the things that a society needs to accomplish on an ongoing, daily basis to survive. What kind of list would we come up with? Well, humans need food, fresh water, the means to effectively take care of their young, systems of travel, shelter, and more. And with each of these basic items we can be increasingly innovative and add conveniences, such as the manner in which we grow or produce food, how rapidly we can access clean water, and the degree of efficiency or luxury in which we control these things. In society, we also need to consider how we interact with each other, how we spend time together, how we protect ourselves from foreign aggressors, and then maybe, even how we protect each other from one another. We need smart people to help construct our written and unwritten rules. We need people individually, in organizations, and in systems of government and business to create a consistency of culture to make all of these things happen. Consider the book or computer from which you are reading. Who designed it? Who assembled it? Where did the materials come from? Who put in the labor? And, most important, how does this product contribute to the betterment of society?

In American society, or American culture, there are formal and informal ways in which we learn. There are the humanities and the sciences, both of which hold necessary roles in society. Creativity in art and language is equally as useful as the formulations that result from computation and engineering. These material and nonmaterial processes are observed in a number of different shapes and forms, as there are many ways in which culture is taught and learned.

Socialization is how "people learn the attitudes, values, and behaviors appropriate for members of a particular culture" (Schaefer 2010:76). One's family is the primary vessel through which socialization begins. The process is internal and people typically are advantaged or disadvantaged respective of the strengths or weaknesses of one's upbringing. This socialization can bestow a status that affords "limitless" or "limited" access and opportunity to the recipient. However, individual curiosity, education, and awareness can open many doors and social pathways, even when an individual starts with very little.

Assimilation, in a broad sense, is the process by which members of a group learn and adapt to the customs, values, and ways of another group or larger society. There is an expectation that the older, larger, or more dominant group will assist the smaller, or minority members, to understand the manner in which society operates. Ultimately, a societal goal is to have the smaller group integrate itself seamlessly with the larger group.

Now, the mere mention of the processes of socialization and assimilation could inspire a separate lecture or essay due to the complex history of America. I say complex because socialization and assimilation refer to the promotion of existing social norms and cultural values. These messages are useful for the integration of society, but it is also the intentional transmission of the dominant culture. Let's not be misled. There are systematic advantages and disadvantages to these processes, depending upon your particular group or context.

Did you take a class in history, civics, or social studies while in school? By any chance, did you take any courses that were specifically focused on African American history or your particular cultural/ethnic history? I would bet that there are not many who have done so. When we talk about the transmission of the dominant culture, we're talking about values that are based on mainstream

American norms. These norms and values, particularly with regard to building history, are delivered through education, so that vital information, as deemed by the dominant culture, is communicated to students for their citizen development. So, knowing about George Washington, Thomas Jefferson, the Constitution and Declaration of Independence is part and parcel of transferring history and culture. And when one thinks about the history that's available through the public school systems, many would consider it devoid of many aspects of minority culture. For instance, the standard delivery of black American culture is typically limited to the era of chattel slavery, Harriet Tubman, and Martin Luther King's "I have a Dream" speech. To meet such deficiencies, during the black power era of the 1960s and 1970s, there were demands from many students for black history courses on college campuses. These students had trouble with the idea of only select people determining the important facts of all of American society. They understood that when a certain aspect of history is deemed more valuable than others, societal division will continue.

For the sake of this broad essay on education and awareness, I will simply assert that socialization and assimilation are the processes by which younger or minority groups are taught how to be citizens by the larger group. These processes are learned through formal education on the history of the society, as well as informally, through nonverbal, yet observable symbols and codes that guide society. In all, the development of competent and aware citizens is the responsibility of the socializers and all who hope to maintain their society.

Who charts the vision or the pathway that a society follows? Well, if a society is sustainable, there usually are systems and processes by which the leadership comes into that position. In American society, there is a process of voting in which eligible citizens vote for a group of leaders. As we know, from observing this country as well as others, the selection of leaders does not always feel like a fair and impartial process. The reasoning stems from the ascribed status that comes along with inclusion in a particular racial and social class. However, as society has evolved, some of the barriers to entry have weakened. This is evidenced with the election of the current president, Barack Obama. So here in America, by and large, our process for governmental leader selection works. It has checks and balances throughout the process. It's certainly not perfect, but most of us accept it without much complaint. With that, we as citizens have the right and, more important, the duty to participate in this leadership selection process and/or to change it. We need competent citizens because we must select leaders who have the concrete and abstract skills necessary to govern our society. In addition to selecting certain leaders, we must not only vote, we also have to be an instrumental part of fulfilling the vision they express.

As the next generation of citizens and leaders, my high school and college students are asked how their personal and career goals contribute to the fulfillment of a better society. Whether in grade school, high school, or at the university level, their job is just that — to acquire knowledge of themselves and the universe. They need to be instructed and guided to learn about their world and society. They must understand that they must either learn how to maintain society or be prepared to change it. One needs to be an aware citizen in order to do either. We need smart people.

CASH AND STATUS

A second reason why education and awareness are vital is because they allow for the possibility of individual upward mobility. In essence, we're talking about how to attain cash and status. The simple thinking behind this point is that if you start at Point A, then it's likely that if you attain the skills and grasp the ideas of society, you should be able to move closer to Point Z more rapidly than someone who doesn't have that education. It's a good bet that 90% of the people on college campuses are there because they want this advantage or leverage. From birth, you have been hearing about the American Dream: that if you work hard and get a good education, you will be able to land a good job and be successful. And, for the most part, this is true. Any research would indicate that the greater percentage of more highly educated folks make more money and are less likely to be unemployed. Furthermore, not only is the job willing to pay you more, but it is often more prestigious than those occupations where fewer skills are required, where there is a salary versus an hourly wage; where there is health coverage versus none; and whether you take a bath at night or in the morning. That last statement is a little levity that addresses the difference between a blue collar worker and white collar worker; a blue collar worker typically takes a bath after they work and the white collar worker takes it in the morning before they work. This example isn't speaking to a negative aspect of blue collar work but is simply recognizing the physical nature of it.

Parents and elders in one's life continuously suggest that once one has an education, no one can take it from them. Even in grade school, folks would elaborate on how valuable education was and that it would be worth the hard work. In the study of sociology, there is a concept called the "human capital" theory. It is the "argument that individuals make investments in their own 'human capital' in order to increase their productivity and earnings" (Giddens et al. 2007:288). So, in the case of a student who stays up late at night working on a paper, or rushes through traffic to make every class, or organizes study groups so they can be best prepared for an examination, they are making an investment in their own self-worth. For these individuals, the stress of the effort is worth the future reward.

The potential benefits of this theory could well manifest themselves on more levels than just academia. This investment is relevant for those who are em-

14

ployed or unemployed or for those simply trying to make it from Point A to Point B. The human capital theory is very much like the idea of physically getting in shape. You run, lift weights, and do sit ups all in the hopes of getting "healthy" or, on a more superficial level, looking good. As soon as they've finished a workout, many folks jump on a scale or look in the mirror to see if the "investment" in their body has begun to pay off. If we see results, then, most times we will continue. If we don't, it becomes a little harder to continue while waiting for the delayed gratification. In today's America, we are a society that struggles with the patience required for development. We want our food cooked (microwaved) in seconds, our information found immediately (e.g. Google), and a wait for anything is unacceptable. Our impatience is often the same with education, particularly for those doing it strictly for upward mobility. The stressors, frustration, and costs feel much greater than what we may have learned or the career or earnings "value" that lies ahead in the future.

But envision this: close your eyes and imagine your graduation ceremony. You're sitting there in your graduation cap and gown, the school official calls your name, and your family and friends begin to scream hysterically, cheering you on. At this moment, you can't deny an ear-to-ear smile. You walk across the stage and you shake the hands of school officials, and the president of the institution places the degree in your hand. How could that feeling be described? Relief? Excitement? Do the words "validated" or "certified" come to mind? Do you all of a sudden feel smart? Maybe. Some actually feel that the ceremony validates all that they have done over the previous years of study. That's why the event or, in particular, the moment, is so important. What has happened is that you have received in your hand a tool that you know will make you valuable in society. This is called *credentialism*. Credentials are the tools you possess that identify you as certified and qualified to participate in a particular area of the job market. Most people come to America strictly for the opportunity of securing American credentialism. If you want to give yourself the best chance of securing stability and success in America, you have to have the credentials that prove, or at least suggest, to people that you know what the hell you're talking about.

The importance of this change in status (and quite possibly, cash/income) is consistent with the principles and ideals of America. An ideal such as "hard work equals success" is part of the larger economic dynamic or framework of the United States, which is capitalism. In an economic or business sense, capitalism merely asserts that you can work to build a business, you provide a quality product or service, and people will spend their money, at your price, if they desire what you have to offer. If they no longer like your product or service, or think it's overpriced, what will happen? It's simple: people will stop buying it. Thus, the consumer forces the supplier to be more innovative in their approach to delivering the product or service, thereby making it of greater quality. All the while, there are several other people/entities in competition with you, trying to make something better. Although some look at the word capitalism as greed-driven and heartless, it's quite a beautiful concept because it simply allows for people to stay motivated and working hard to provide society with the next best "thing."

In a social sense, people often fear capitalism because it is believed that individuals are self-centered toward their own goals and profit. People fear that it creates less "human-centered" societies. Well, I ask, what makes "capitalists" any different from kids who are on campuses all across America, drinking coffee to stay awake, struggling to pay tuition, doing late nights in the library, reading exam review notes for the next class all while multitasking on something else? It's all because they want to get ahead in life. There is nothing wrong with fulfilling the human capital theory. I, like most others who are honest in their thinking, would much rather prefer to be a "have" than a "have not" so let's not deny our individual ambitions. It's a tough world out here and in order to be a winner we have to bite, scratch, and claw to present ourselves as a "quality product" in order to survive and access upward mobility.

I personally believe capitalism is innate. It's instinctive. This is the reason why the guiding rule of all religious texts focuses on "being kind to one's neighbor" simply so we don't eliminate all humanity in our individual quests. But, at the same time, we must acknowledge that the big fish will eat the little fish ... unless the little fish is smart enough to avoid being eaten. What are you doing to avoid being eaten by the big fish? This is very much a type of social Darwinism in that one understands that one must leverage one's strengths in order to survive and succeed. Maybe, we can begin to call Darwin's theory "Survival — and Success — of the Fittest." We must consider upward mobility for what it is — a chance to survive and succeed.

CHANGE AND SUCCESS

Now that we have talked about two different elements of education, let's conclude with one final function. The last purpose of education is to liberate people from the bonds of ignorance (Lauer and Lauer 2013:322). Now, in reading this, one may come to a number of conclusions. Some may say that it is an obvious statement. Others may look for a deeper and more personal, as well as social, application of it. Thinking on that level will allow one to see that this statement is more about individual change and success and how those two aspirations can lead to contributions on a broader level. Let me explain.

One of the first things that comes to mind is to decipher some of the language of the statement. Let's work backwards. What is ignorance? By definition, ignorance is "showing or having little knowledge or awareness" (Merriam Webster Dictionary 2013). What that means is that one's ability to be aware of self and society is very limited. Being ignorant is often a tragic consequence of up-bringing and inequality, but it could also be self-imposed. What I'm suggesting is that some people are not interested in developing any further, advancing their own worth, or putting forth any effort to do better. So, in essence, they are ignorant to their own ignorance. Follow me?

Now, a bond is something that keeps two things together. When something is stuck, taped, or fastened together, it can eventually come apart. But the word "bond" suggests that there is almost a natural symmetry between two things. In this instance, I'll examine people and ignorance, or, better yet, the connection or symmetry allowing for the bond of human apathy and ignorance to exist. I see one aspect of the human condition as powerful, motivated, and driven. However, I see the alternate half as weak, apathetic, and depressed. There are those who are born leaders and those who are groomed followers. On the periphery are the conditions that can impact our human response to this bond. To find our greatest self worth, we must aspire beyond any bonds of limitation.

Lastly, what does liberate mean? Well, liberate means to completely free someone or something from a hindrance in their life. It means freedom in every sense of the word. One is not confined or restricted to any particular dominant person, force, or, more importantly, set of ideas. Liberated means free to pursue one's own unique agenda and priorities in life. It means the freedom to be one's own intellectual, emotional, and social authority. In great part, it means the ability to define oneself.

In reflection, the first function of education teaches about culture and society. In the second, we focused on upward mobility and economic sustainability. I see this last function or element as most vital because it is all about finding the best of oneself. This element is really about the old, traditional adage: "Know thyself" and, as an unknown writer once said, "Once we learn ourselves, all learning becomes fun because we have already mastered one discipline." This axiom is relevant here, as the beginning stages of true freedom provide the ability to exist within or alter any dynamic offered in society. This liberation is exempt of the "teacher expectancy" effect, in which people learn, based on the high or low the expectations of their teacher. That expectation is necessary for those unmotivated by learning. But, when one pursues or attains knowledge of self, no other sources are needed for learning. Once one learns one's self, the possibility for constructive, personal, and social contributions is endless.

This liberation can be complemented with Abraham Maslow's theoretical construct about humans "Hierarchy of Needs." McLeod (2014) notes that Maslow created a pyramid shaped structure wherein he identified certain human needs. The most basic needs (physiological, esteem, belonging) were at the bottom, widest point of the pyramid and the top of the pyramid was a point of self-actualization or what some consider to be personal success and fulfillment. Maslow's construct deemed it necessary to meet the lower level needs of the pyramid in order to reach the top. He studied leaders and thinkers such as Frederick Douglass, Eleanor Roosevelt, and Albert Einstein to examine what made them exemplary. From their examples, he was able to see that it was crucial for these lower levels to be met before they could ascend to the highest level. This theory aligns with this essay in that the first two functions of education represent how we maintain the lower levels of the pyramid. Liberating oneself from the bonds of ignorance is reaching the highest level of self-actualization.

To examine this on a more personal level, self-actualization or knowing oneself is about those mornings when you wake up and you feel good about the day.

19

Have you ever had those days when you just feel great, all is sunny outside, and you just feel in harmony with God? You're happy about learning, going to school or work, and the people in your life have made you smile. On a social or, let's say, professional level, reaching self-actualization is finding your ultimate calling. Everyone has a skill, strength, or major area of interest that they presumably desire to translate into a professional passion. With the education one acquires, the goal has to be to make a "splash" when entering one's area of expertise. That's all a part of self-actualization. It's about the journey of learning yourself, the world, and challenging yourself to reach a place of contentment every day. Some days are harder than others, but education and awareness, formal and informal, can take you there. That's liberation.

So, should a parent or the president of your country have to motivate you to pursue your highest self? This motivational push comes because there is a firm understanding amongst the elder generation that one's experience toward awareness has an impact not only on the individual, but for the larger society as well. I would like to argue that one element has a greater value than another, but I believe that call is made on a person-by-person basis. I do, however, know that one's self-liberation is important to any type of learning about other people, things, or ideas. You must understand yourself in any effort to impact society. Status can be bestowed on you but achieved status is doubly gratifying. This awareness, this consciousness, is not only what drives our formal knowledge, but it also transforms our abstract ideas into tangible action. By creating your value, you not only change your life for the better, but, you can also change the world.

Queens **broken** underestimated **STRO**

ORANT undervalued RESILIENT Violent Marginalized CREATIVE *Lazy*

itual Dependent OPPRESSED Smart *Confused* Free athletic

ponsible **LOUD** Articulate THUG Brilliant inferior KING

vative Artistic REGAL *Queens* **broken** underestir

TRONG IGNORANT undervalued RESILIENT Violent Ma

ATIVE *Lazy* Conditioned *Spiritual* Dependent OPPRESSED Smart C

etic Stupid Irresponsible **LOUD** Articulate THUG Brillia

NGS slaves Innovative Artistic REGAL *Queens* **broke**

derestimated **STRONG** IGNORANT undervalued

lent Marginalized CREATIVE *Lazy* Conditioned *Spiritual* Dependent

rt *Confused* Free athletic Stupid Irresponsible **LOUD** A

IUG Brilliant inferior KINGS slaves Innovative Artistic REG

Queens **broken** underestimated **STRO**

ORANT undervalued RESILIENT Violent Marginalized CREATIVE *Lazy*

itual Dependent OPPRESSED Smart *Confused* Free athletic

AMERICAN COSTUMES

[THE PERVASIVE IDEA OF RACE IN OUR SOCIETY]

As humans, and particularly Americans, are we savvy enough to talk about the topic of "race" without talking about "race-ism?" Are we in a position in the United States of America where we can sit down in racially mixed company and have a civil conversation about the topic? Can one just say, "Please share more about your race but do not include any qualifiers that suggest power or inequality?" Unfortunately, I don't think we can. In this essay I'll explain my dismay and why race is such a divisive topic.

One of the unfortunate realities woven into American history and culture is our loyalty to physical differences and the resultant consequences of those realities. In America, race is a very deep-seated, emotional idea that unfortunately, at the surface, is merely stereotypical labeling and name-calling. Although ridden with surface critiques, it remains a pervasive idea because there is power associated with race. We can vehemently disagree or naively ignore the power scale, but if it were ultimately irrelevant, I wouldn't be writing this and you wouldn't be reading it. Allow me to clarify with a few observations.

In many human circles, the topic of race is always abuzz. People can talk about gender inequality or poverty and could note some of the huge disparities in the way people are treated personally, professionally, and socially. But, somehow, those topics feel a little lighter than a discussion revolving around race. Race seems to always catch us in our most vulnerable positions and strike at our most delicate emotions. Why is that?

I'll begin by suggesting that this country was built on the visible differences of race. The difference between race and the other distinctive forms of inequality is that race should have no tangible value on sight ... but it does. For instance, if one is rich or poor or if we highlight the physical differences between men and women, it is clear how those differences could suggest power in society. When one is poor, it may be visually evident that they are in a position of need and have obvious limitations due to their plight. The same goes with physical differences between the sexes, in that men are typically bigger, stronger, and faster than women and those differences are often assumed to translate into a greater capacity for labor or production. However, race carries its own status as many of the notions associated with power are not physically obvious but, unfortunately, ascribed and assumed. Whether it's intellectual capacity, economic sustainability, or professional status, value is often assigned based on racial history, not on any specific limitations or capabilities of the human being.

I'll elaborate on this idea later in the essay, but I want first to establish a greater structure for this conversation. Looking at many of the key notions associated with the topic, I believe it's important that we're clear and of the same under-standing as we move forward. When we talk about inequality among the races, we must decipher the nuances in terminology and the tangents that don't make good sense for a productive discussion. We need to examine what these quali-fiers are and make sure that we're using them appropriately when we're trying to argue or present a position on this topic.

WHEN IS IT REALLY RACISM?

If racism really exists, can you prove it? As one considers that point, try to avoid the many subjective instances that may run through your mind. For instance, if I am Person A of one race and you are Person B of another, and I appear to be following you around my store, is that based on race? If I cross the street as I see you and a group of your friends walking in the opposite direction on the same street, am I now a racist? If I get pulled over late at night by a police officer of another race, while other cars seemingly zoom by, was that encounter based on race? See, with all of the instances above, depending on your race, you may have said yes or no. Each human and the varied history of each racial group may lead to several different responses to those scenarios. In an effort to avoid debat-ing the matter, I'm looking for the most concrete instances to prove racism. We want to avoid personal opinion and subjectivity. If it's so pervasive, then why is it often a challenge to prove?

Now, the obvious instances of racism are when we can refer to humans who are directly affiliated to a group (Ku Klux Klan, Skinheads, Neo-Nazis, etc.) for whom part of its creed and mission is that of disdain for other races and consider them inferior. In an instance of asking my students about contemporary and ob-vious racism, they brought up the 2009 shooting at the United States Holocaust

Memorial Museum by a man whose past is associated with racist groupings. That was a clear example of one who, driven by racial hatred, executed a particular crime in society. That type of hate is substantial and concrete. At the same time, it was an isolated instance. So, if racism exists, wouldn't these situations happen every day? I think some would suggest that the reality of racial hate is waning and that that is why you see fewer instances of overt and profound hate.

What I'm looking to discuss are systemic issues such as any federal or state laws, policies, or specific practices that state, or even suggest, that a certain "race" of people can't legally do something that another group can. What information, specifically, in the Constitution, the Bill of Rights, or any legal documents allows for a hierarchy to be established amongst racial groups? After a casual or thorough analysis of the country's framing documents and/or current laws and policies, I think, in 2015, it's quite evident that there is little to no language or verbiage that suggests anything but equality and freedom. In fact, some of the mainstream culture may suggest that there is more language of "reverse racism" in our laws. This idea is based on the notion that there are hiring practices or, for instance, college admissions requirements that are beneficial for minorities to the exclusion of possibly more qualified candidates of another race or the white majority. It is a messy web to weave but still a valid position to consider. Many would argue that our justice system has clear tactics that disproportionately, negatively impact people of color. These are debates that could go on for days. The bottom line I'm trying to establish is the fact that much of our thinking about race is subjective; the process of identifying substantial evidence that racism exists as a policy of the nation can be an elusive exercise.

FACTS ABOUT RACE

Ok, so let's dig deeper ... what is race? Most people would say it is the difference between people based on the color of their skin. But, with so many hues, the range of complexion between many within one particular racial group can be staggering. So, technically defined, "race is a group of persons related by common descent or heredity" (Lauer and Lauer 2013:228). With this definition in mind, and the numerous divisions of humankind based on heredity, it seems difficult to maintain what is pure and homogenous. I assert that what race is composed of in modern society is actually arbitrary and based on false presumptions.

Now an ethnic group is "a people who have a shared historical and cultural background that leads them to identify with each other" (Lauer and Lauer 2013:227). In more detail, ethnicity is composed of the characteristics of a group whose members share a common cultural heritage, a sense of "peoplehood" that they pass from one generation to the next. So ethnicity is more cultural, whereas race is "perceived" to be more biological. Based on appearances or the way one looks is the way we choose to define where a particular person fits racially. The determination of these observations is becoming more and more difficult in American society. There is no science or formula that allows one to determine to which category people belong. When you have a mixture, and miscegenation, if you will, the combining of races with black and Hispanic, black and white, white and Hispanic, white and Asian, etc., ... there's this melting pot effect that's taking place, which is blurring the lines of how we visually define race. It's interesting though, in that the darker you are on the visual continuum, the greater your challenges may still be today.

Many citizens in the Unites States aren't able to make a close estimation of how race is broken down by percentage in America. For instance, if we had to guess out of 100 people in the United States, many would struggle to determine the number or percentage of those who are identified as black, white, Asian, Hispanic, or other. Interestingly, it's where you live within the country that will probably determine your answer to this question. In 2010, the demographics in terms of statistical percentage, blacks would account for about 13%, white non-Hispanic around 66%, Hispanic 14%, Asian and other 5%, while American Indian is 2% (Schaefer 2010:238). What may be interesting is the near extinction of American Indians in a land that was once theirs ... but, we'll save that for another conversation.

What becomes confusing for folks oftentimes is that depending on where they live, they envision the rest of the country in that manner. For instance, if you live in the heartland of the United States and don't see black Americans regularly, you may fall victim to the impression that blacks are an insignificant minority. Conversely, if you live on the east coast, from north to south, you could make the assumption that blacks are a larger part of the nationwide population than they actually are. But for a sense of fairness to be achieved, the key factors on the table are not the everyday, commonplace visual reminders of race but the systemic reminders of equality or inequality. Based on these demographic percentages, one needs merely to explore all the groups' roles in media, government, and Wall Street to determine if there is fair representation of races in this American melting pot.

Looking into the future of racial demographics, an understanding of the angst of American cultural change becomes evident. For instance, if we look at the demographics projected for the year 2100, white non-Hispanics will decrease from

66% to 40%, Hispanics will go from 14% to 33%, Asians and other populations will grow slightly, and the percentage of black Americans is projected to stay relatively the same (Schaefer 2010:238). So, Hispanic, Asian, and other populations look to grow, whereas black Americans and white non-Hispanics will either stay the same or decrease. These "visual" numbers have ramifications for a lot of symbolic as well as public policy decisions that take place in society and for those who makes those decisions. From a cultural perspective of the country, many are concerned about the changes that this racially diverse society could bring. Former presidential candidate and conservative political pundit Pat Buchanan has written extensively about the impact of a changing American culture in his book, *State of Emergency*. Buchanan (2006:11) writes, "America faces an existential crisis. If we do not get control of our borders, by 2050 Americans of European descent will be a minority in the nation their ancestors created and built."

Current President Barack Obama understands that the nation is changing and that his melting pot effect is taking place. The melting pot is essentially the amalgamation of society where there is a fine blending of colors and cultures. What better example than he, as he is a product of a biracial union? With the racial history of this country, it is quite a compliment to some, and tragedy to others, that we now have a biracial citizen in the highest office in the land. Let's be honest, if you look at those who have been in office since the founding of the United States, this is a challenging optic in some folks' minds. It is easy to understand how changes in demographic variance mean the power to vote, power to support, and power to control. For many, it may be alarming that the way the country has operated for the last 200 plus years is changing. While this changing view remains terrifying for many, it is encouraging to the rest. Race as a visual codifier has a very powerful impact.

As I mentioned earlier, racism is the belief that some races are inherently inferior to others. The key word in this definition is belief. So, substantiating how racism exists is a challenging task because that existence is a system based on beliefs. In fact, the word "prejudice" is usually attached to the word "racial." Racial prejudice is a pattern of thinking about another person based on observable racial differences. On the other hand, when we talk about discrimination, we begin to discuss acts that impact other individuals based on prejudice. Discrimination "the actions, the policies and the practices that deny an individual or group equal access to societies, resources and opportunities" (Schaefer 2010:241) is completely different from prejudice. So, racial prejudice is a biased belief system and racial discrimination is the actual actions, policies, and practices that deny people certain access to opportunities and privileges in society.

In that we can all clearly understand the nuances of race, those instances of "I was in the store and somebody followed me around" or "The teacher gave me a bad grade on my test because I'm ..." are all instances of what is called stealth racism. Stealth racism is "the hidden or subtle acts of prejudice and discrimination that may be apparent only to the victim" (Lauer and Lauer 2013:243). So, in these cases, could these examples of mistreatment have been some type of prejudice or discriminatory behavior? Quite possibly. As individuals, we can't change the negative perceptions that we believe someone may have of us. The more concrete and impactful form of racism to be concerned with is systemic and/or "institutional racism" and that is what must be eliminated from society. Institutional racism is defined as the "policies and practices of social institutions that tend to perpetuate racial discrimination" (Lauer and Lauer 2013:243). I have noted two different types of racial behavior. The responses to such racial behaviors are the cause for continued confusion and mistreatment in society.

RACE AS AN IDEA

Having explored both stealth and institutional racism, the most captivating thing that I have discovered about the topic of race is that it is merely an idea. Now, some may ask, "What in the world does that mean?" What the statement means is that race is a social, not necessarily biological, construction which characterizes and categorizes groups of people by superficial physical observations. What most don't understand is that external physical differences, or similarities, have nothing to do with our internal genetic make-up as human beings. What one sees on the outside may have no genetic, intellectual, or physical consistency with someone else who looks similar. Race is just an idea.

Let's start from the beginning; when you think about race, what is it? Why are we categorized by race? How is it that individuals are categorized in society by race? What is biologically different or similar about different races of human beings? A simple fact is that the only way to truly determine race is through eye shape, hair texture, and skin color. Other than that there is nothing biological about race. Yes, this is true! So everything that has been ascribed to different racial groups is just a social definition that has been assigned to them. The ability to produce melanin, or pigmentation, is one of the only, but obviously key differences, amongst certain groups of humans. There is nothing biological, however, that says that one group is intellectually inferior or physically superior to another. There is no biological trait that can be traced to particular strengths or deficits in one particular group. With this being mentioned, it's easier to understand what is meant when one states that race is simply an idea.

If there are no distinct internal similarities between the races, the value in chunking people into categories must be examined. Because of the obvious external similarities, it makes it quite easy to believe — no critical thinking involved — that people who look similar are the same. The Eugenics movement of the early 20th century sought to ascribe genetic superiority and inferiority to the construct of race, thereby casting people of the darkest hue to the bottom of the social hierarchy. Therefore, if some individuals think or behave one particular way, it will be assumed that that behavior is associated with that particular race. And, conversely, if they are of one particular race, then they must behave in one particular way. When you look at DNA, however, none of the social cues or meanings that we attribute to race apply. Not one. Think about how we have come to understand black, think about how we have come to understand Hispanic, think about how we have come to understand Asian, think about how we have come to understand white … now, erase it from your mind because none of it is true. It's a belief system. It's a belief, it's constructed, and there's nothing biological about it. Fruit flies appear identical but have a million more differences among them than humans do.

THE COSTUME AND ITS CONSEQUENCE

Besides your hair texture, the shape of your eyes, and the color of your skin, what else makes you uniquely black, white, Hispanic, or Asian? Is there anything? Can you say I dance better because I'm black? If I suggest that then that means that all black people should be able to say that. And is that true? No, it's not. Do you have a unique aptitude or an understanding for engineering or science because you're Asian? Were you born that way? Is there anything that is specific to any racial category besides those three external physical differences mentioned? There is nothing.

I hypothesize in the title of this chapter the idea that race can be seen as a costume. In actuality, each human costume has little to no value; however, different levels of value have been assigned to the costumes. Within this example, there's the belief that one's costume breeds an inherent superiority, inferiority, or set of behaviors that are genetically based. The truth is that the costume is just a costume and most traits or behaviors are part of a socialized culture. For instance, some folks, from when they were little kids ate chicken, macaroni, and collard greens. The food is part of a cultural construct not a racial one. It's something that one learned, not something that came as a matter of instinct. Another example is that if you dance, hunt, or speak better than some, it's probably because you learned it, not that the quality or talent is something you were born with due to your race. Similarly, people don't pick up certain language characteristics because they're genetically inherent to one group of people. These are all learned behaviors. So if you put a white kid in a black family and he grows up with that family, I argue he would be able to speak and perform all the things that any other black kid can do because he was socialized within that culture. In short, nearly everything we mention as associated with race should be appropriately defined as culture.

Hopefully you have been able to gain a sense of what is myth and what is fact with regard to race. Historically, due to the myths and facts of race, some individuals were granted privileges, while others were denied access to certain privileges. These choices impact the circumstances of one's reality and ultimate ability to succeed in the present or build in the future. In the groundbreaking documentary, *Race: The Power of an Illusion* (2003), the post-World War II era is highlighted, in which an aspect of the aforementioned reality is illustrated, where only whites were given home loans through the federal government. Blacks were not permitted access to loans in certain areas thereby causing two different standards of living for blacks and whites. Ultimately, in 1968, Lyndon Johnson signed the Fair Housing Act that eliminated the language in a government document that blocked blacks from buying in particular areas. The change in this institutionally discriminatory practice provided an opportunity for all minorities to have access to a standard of living that they could afford and that they desired. In terms of race relations, this was a moment of great optimism for minorities in this country.

Unfortunately, what would appear to be a governmental and social trajectory toward equality did not necessarily materialize. Once minorities began pursuing homeownership in predominantly white areas, the whites would start to leave. A simple change in law did not change the myths and perceptions about the value of different racial groups or "costumes." During that time, and even today, homeownership was a key to establishing economic viability, and oftentimes, wealth. There was a material profit analysis that would be made based on practices that inflated the value of white neighborhoods and diminished the value of black communities. Real estate developers would pose the scenario to white homeowners: "Blacks are moving to this neighborhood and it's getting ready to change. Your house ... I know it's worth $100,000 but I'm going to give you $80,000. You better take it right now because the value's going to continue to decrease" (Adelman et al. 2003). Many whites, fearful of the drop in property values due to the perceived inferior value of black humanity, would leave these communities with less than what their homes were worth. So, these block-busting practices would then lead to investors buying a home in a white community for $80,000 and, simultaneously, sell it for $120,000 to the blacks trying to move into the once white, suburban neighborhood. By playing on the fear of racial differences, investors made tons of money. Based on a perceived racial idea that certain groups were inferior and others were superior, the color and economic value of entire neighborhoods were changed. The true concern in this scenario is that "white flight" is a reaction that many would argue still happens today. This dynamic is moderately compromised as some of America has matured racially: divisions are less likely drawn along racial lines but more so along economic ones.

W.E.B. Du Bois observed this reality of color as early as the turn of the 20th Century. He spoke in detail of the problem of the color line in his work, *Souls of Black Folks* ([1903]1995). His ideas are still relevant because if I were to name any geographic locale in an area, most people are able to tell where the neighborhood changes along the lines of race and/or economics. People's lives are determined as a result of the idea that race has value and oftentimes the people's home value is deflated or inflated as a result. Now, I'm talking about households having different access to resources and amenities and the value margin being the difference among schools, safety, and savings. One's entire quality of life is impacted by a perception. Most American households' wealth is in the form of home ownership. So if you have a $300,000 house and you want to take out a $50,000 home equity loan to send your child to college, the equity allows you to pass that money on to the next generation. This could be the beginning of what is called "generational wealth." Now, if you rent or your house isn't worth as much as it might be because of its location, you can't pass that money on, so that wealth or the sustainability factor is impeded.

Another honest revelation of our racial costumes is that there's a tipping point in each community. Once minorities move into a predominately white neighborhood and, as Malcolm Gladwell (2002) suggests, become more than 20-25% of that particular neighborhood, folks may begin to see that phenomenon of white flight again. See, some feel that diversity and visual pluralism is a really cool thing as long as it is controlled and limited. Once diversity hits its peak of 20-25%, it's time to consider a change as the value in quality-of-life matters may be altered due to the perception of a minority-heavy area. As I mentioned earlier, white flight is dissipating due to loose immigration practices and growing minority groups. But, let's not be mistaken, the flight takes place — even when folks look alike — when major cultural or economic changes feel imminent. In the future, I suspect it will be very hard to find homogenous, white areas, so the impact of white flight will be diluted. Economic differentiations will be the guiding force as to how communities and quality-of-life matters are constructed.

GIVING ALL COSTUMES VALUE

In a society built on an economic framework of capitalism, money will always organize society and how we perceive and define it. With the influx and growing trend of wealthy, gifted, and successful people of color, race will become only a visual reminder of where the country has come from. On the other side, color will continue to represent the worst of society due to stealth assumptions and institutional reactions to race. At the end of the day, there's a sociological concept known as the "contact hypothesis" that states that in "cooperative circumstances, interracial contact between people of equal status will cause them to become less prejudice and to abandon old stereotypes" (Schaefer 2013:246). I completely agree with this notion as relevant to where we are in race relations in America. As more and more people have the opportunity to interact with one another and learn that there aren't as many differences that we perceive in our minds, then racial equality begins to take shape. The key is that we all have to be willing to push the dialogue. We have to stop looking for the commonality of race and begin to expand our human interaction to respect and appreciate culture.

Through the contact hypothesis, people will learn the facts that groups of people are different based off of a few small characteristics, nothing internal, and nothing biological, just a few external physical characteristics. As society continues to grow and generations of children grow further removed from the racial tensions of their parents' and grandparents' past, society becomes more and more comfortable with human differences. The optics of the Obama family era push this discussion even further into the depths of our consciousness. As an example, my children are growing up with the only president they have ever known being a black American.

Our differences can be celebrated by an appreciation of cultures. The conversation of race only takes us back to the topic of racism. I'm optimistic that my children will grow up in a slightly more mature society that hopefully defines its humanity based on the merit of one's work. The breaking down of these social ideas and the perceived and tangible value associated with them leads us all to a better, more equitable society. Our awareness and interaction on this topic changes the paradigm. It just takes time … yet those who suffer because of their costume are exhausted by the wait.

Queens Broken underestimated STRO

ORANT undervalued RESILIENT Violent Marginalized CREATIVE Lazy

itual Dependent OPPRESSED Smart Confused Free athletic

ponsible LOUD Articulate THUG Brilliant inferior KING

vative Artistic REGAL Queens Broken underestir

TRONG IGNORANT undervalued RESILIENT Violent Ma

ATIVE Lazy Conditioned Spiritual Dependent OPPRESSED Smart c

etic Stupid Irresponsible LOUD Articulate THUG Brillia

NGS slaves Innovative Artistic REGAL Queens Broke

erestimated STRONG IGNORANT undervalued

Lent Marginalized CREATIVE Lazy Conditioned Spiritual Dependen

rt Confused Free athletic Stupid Irresponsible LOUD A

IUG Brilliant inferior KINGS slaves Innovative Artistic REG

Queens Broken underestimated STRO

ORANT undervalued RESILIENT Violent Marginalized CREATIVE Lazy

itual Dependent OPPRESSED Smart Confused Free athletic

THE PECULIAR SYMBOL
[A SOCIOLOGICAL ANALYSIS OF THE ELECTION]
OF PRESIDENT BARACK OBAMA

At one time, I attempted to articulate that blacks in the United States of America had, and always will have, a perpetual status as second tier citizens. By this I meant two things. One, blacks are approximately 13% of the nation's population and thus can only expect proportional representation in the economy, politics, and any other element of society that is vital to America's overall welfare. This 13% will always be a minority, or second tier citizens, I explained, and by their sheer number, they would have to accept their proportional limitations. Two, the term second tier citizen spoke to those who had little to no chance to pursue and win positions of national leadership that would have a tangible and lasting impact on America. I asserted that national leadership seemed unattainable; thus, the humble cloak of fact acceptance was worn by the black race.

I recognized that outside the realm of nationwide leadership, many black Americans had climbed the mountain of equality as it relates to executive employment, exorbitant salaries, lavish homes, and social status. The record of society sup-

41

ported that equality had come for some black Americans in the form of dollar signs and social standing, but the true and more influential elements of national power had remained an elusive aspiration for minorities. Black minorities were aware that a better understanding or some level of attainment of actual political power was critical to their livelihoods. This attainment was imperative because to make America a more inclusive society, a thorough examination must be undertaken of who it is that makes the laws, policies, and decisions that affect the Americans who are responsible for following them.

Then came Barack Obama.

President Barack Obama has crafted the notion that visionary idealism, broad intellectualism, national leadership, and arguably, global leadership, are qualities or traits that any person can pursue, and possess, even as a minority. Obama, a biracial male who identifies himself as black or African American, born of a white American mother and African Kenyan father, has challenged America to make good on its highest ideals. Before his moment, society felt comfortable not questioning whether the fusion of power politics, intellectual thought, and vision was a playground restricted solely for white, Anglo-Saxon, Protestant males. In this essay, I analyze the symbolic significance of Barack Obama's election to the presidency of the United States of America.

Obama's candidacy was a reflection of the three core sociological theories. It is necessary to eloquently capture and analyze this moment, as it will not be President Obama's work as the leader of the free world for which he will be remembered. His most significant contribution will be the climactic moments of American idealism that took place throughout his campaign and reached its initial apex on November 4, 2008. This essay, clearly written from the perspective of examining social reality, will dissect that momentous occasion in American history. It will describe and speak from the functionalist state that Americans have settled for, the conflicting expression of change from the masses, and the true symbolic authentication of the Constitution and promise of the United States that all men are created equal.

FUNCTIONALIST PERSPECTIVE

In America, race has always been a subject that has come under scrutiny. Events such as slavery, the Civil War, and the Civil Rights movement were all periods in which the topic of race drew considerable attention, albeit under very contentious circumstances. Attempts to objectively discuss, comprehend, and neutralize the complexity of this elephant in the room never truly surfaced as individuals typically perceived their subjective understanding of the topic as correct. Everyone in America is an expert on race … or so they believe. The fact of the matter is that many have believed that race was a biological or physical phenomenon that required little to understand. Because of the racial history of America, it was commonly understood that white meant pure, clean, and presumably superior, whereas black came to be known as dark, wicked, and "less than." The ideas of inferiority and superiority were taken as fact and mainstream thought was never overtaken by logic. The exceptions were the independent thinkers who sought to challenge these notions and question the assumed superiority or inferiority of any human being. In these progressive circles, the fact that race is merely a social construct has long existed. But, like slavery, it was understood that the American race dynamic was a brilliant, yet peculiar, institutional idea to codify humans with an ascribed status based on their physical characteristics. A means of oppression, race was used to justify the dehumanization of minorities in America.

With further analysis from the subjects of oppression and those curiously outside of its sphere, race came to be recognized as useful to maintain a concentrated center of power and marginalize the minorities who were not part of the dominant group. For clarification, Richard Schaefer (2010) defines minority:

> When sociologists define a minority group, they are concerned primarily with the economic and political power, or powerlessness, of that group. A minority group is a subordinate group whose members have significantly less control or power over their own lives than the members of a dominant or majority group have over theirs. (P. 237)

Wielding little power, minority cultures struggled and sought to identify their homogenous identity within the heterogeneous ideals of America. This posed a challenge as true assimilation "is the process through which a person forsakes his or her own cultural tradition to become part of a different culture" (Schaefer 2010:248). The national or dominant culture of America supported minority endeavors within certain parameters as there are many definitions of proper assimilation. These parameters could always be enforced by any number of overt, or covert, measures of racism, prejudice, and injustice. With this paradigm, the minority idea was not something that should be expanded into certain political and economic realms. The goal of the dominant in America was for minority assimilation not pluralism and amalgamation.

The functionalist thinker understands that the process of assimilation is necessary for social stability but discounts the conflict of identity it produces for the black as well as minority citizen. Sociologist W.E.B. Du Bois asserted in the early 20th century that the problem in America is the problem of the color line. What Du Bois desired to express was the idea that blacks and other minority races, were bound to a state of *double consciousness*: a state of thinking where it was necessary to assimilate into American culture while attempting to maintain one's independent cultural identity. Du Bois ([1903] 1995) writes:

> It is a peculiar sensation, this double-consciousness, this sense of always looking at one's self through the eyes of others, of measuring one's soul by the tape of a world that looks on in amused contempt and pity. One ever feels his two-ness,—an American, a Negro; two souls, two thoughts, two unreconciled strivings; two warring ideals in one dark body, whose dogged strength alone keeps it from being torn asunder. (P. 45)

In this passage, Du Bois is speaking to the identity crisis that black Americans have long toiled with as they attempted to be true to their culture as well as to America. This unfortunate tension has become a tad less apparent since Du Bois' time as the melting pot grew and social diversity came to be an increasingly functional aspect of America. Even with this growing trend of inclusiveness, the pathways to true power-sharing were incredibly narrow and complex to navigate. The values and ideas that were standards for society remained unrepresentative of all the people. These standards were the ideas that lead to the misguided thinking, suggesting an innate inferiority, or superiority, in human beings. These values determined who was morally upright and who was socially backwards and ignorant. In fact, they still do. Obama challenges this dynamic as the identity crisis arguably lessened because of his ascension to the highest office in the land. In turn, blacks and minorities are optimistic because they feel that a representation of their opinions and ideas is now on the table. Moreover, not only are ideas from someone who battled through this identity crisis on the table, they are in fact guiding the discussion.

A functionalist view of society or any organization, particularly a nation such as the United States, dictates that the numerous dependent and independent parts of society must work together to ensure social stability. For example, the perspective of "division of labor" as articulated by Emile Durkheim suggests the usefulness of work for American social and economic stability. Durkheim argued that there had to exist a natural and organic solidarity in the realms of politics, religion, family, and education. This solidarity allowed for the entities of "society to work in harmony with one another and function as an integrated whole. The continuation of society depends on cooperation, which in turn presumes a general consensus, or agreement, among its members over basic values and customs" (Giddens et al. 2007:14). An unfortunate part of the history of America has been an acceptance of the dominant status quo that has largely excluded the minority opinion from general consensus.

A fortunate functionalist repercussion of Obama's rise to the presidency is that the tangible stability that Americans depend on has not been disrupted. The processes, rhetoric, and challenges of American political life all remained fairly consistent during his campaign. Race became an issue during the primary season; however, it was partially muted by Obama's speech on race and his poise to stay on task of what policies are best for the continuation of a strong country. In the general election, the most intense threat of his opposition came not because of his race or with claims of affiliations with religious extremists or domestic terrorists. Obama's competitors' charges of his being a socialist, one who would entirely alter capitalism and the way America works economically, would have been enough to derail him had his opposition pursued that allegation earlier. Without this alleged threat being firmly established, the assurance of the continuation of American social norms and necessities allowed for stability and avoidance of anomie, the state of confusion that comes as a result of functional disruption.

Barack Obama's ability to uphold the functional apparatus that keeps traditional American politics intact, while challenging the underlying notions of division and inadequacy, is what led to his victory. He silenced the status quo thinking and convinced open minds that a change to inclusivity is useful for the progression of the nation. Even as a young politician and statesman, Obama understood the theory of functionalist thinkers. This quote by Anthony Giddens (2007) sums up what Obama must already have known:

> The functionalist approach holds that if an aspect of social life does not contribute to a society's stability or survival — if it does not serve some identifiably useful function or promote value consensus among members of a society — it will not be passed on from one generation to the next." (P. 15)

This speaks volumes to this present moment at which status quo thinking and racial division appear increasingly useless for American progression. Some now believe the prism of pluralism will lead to the betterment of the country.

SYMBOLIC INTERACTIONIST PERSPECTIVE

Race and symbolism have always been critical topics because America has socialized citizens to attribute a level of truth and belief to their visual and unchallenged orientation and assumptions. See, when one thinks of symbolic interactionism, they cannot limit themselves to words, language, and verbal and nonverbal interactions. An example by the prominent sociologist George Herbert Mead is useful for detail, as he asserts that "when we can think of a tree even if none is visible; we have learned to think of the object symbolically. Symbolic thought frees us from being limited in our experience to what we actually see, hear, or feel" (Giddens et al. 2007:18). The shared social meanings of what humans see is at least equal to what humans say or do.

In this section, I will examine the visual and the verbal. I begin with the word "change." In its simplest form, it means different or to make different. For Barack

Obama, the use of the word as a noun symbolically came to define "him" and as a verb change meant to "make politics different." He was able to capture in the collective consciousness of the American people that his vision symbolized change no matter how they chose to perceive it — as a noun or verb. Standing alone or in conjunction with other words, "change" became a positive descriptor of this new face and phase of American politics. These six letters have been beautifully utilized for their abstract and active qualities, all while providing optimism for those that desired a new direction in America. The word or, should I say, concept, proved to be the most useful slogan in the recent history of presidential political rhetoric.

Visually, as a minority figure, although Obama's glorious ascension may appear as a dramatic first, there have been many who have provided the symbolic visualization necessary for his image not to appear as an outrageous anomaly. Let's return for a moment to the 1930s, when the assumptions on the ground of black athletic ability were limited in scope. A man by the name of Jesse Owens shocked the world by proving himself superior on the track and field defeating any other human being he competed against in the 1936 Olympics in Berlin, Germany. Challenging injustice within his own homeland and being chastised as an inferior athletic specimen abroad by the likes of Adolf Hitler, Owens not only proved himself qualified, but exceeded all expectations of success. Believing that Owens could succeed was one thing; however, seeing him succeed was another. Very much like Owens, Obama's defeat of a national, and global, notion that a minority is incapable of winning the presidency is symbolism for the ages.

To further contextualize this point, we must consider specifically the role of other black political figures. For instance, Shirley Chisholm, and even more so, Jesse Jackson, Sr., had presidential runs that were useful for invigorating black communities and bringing the position of the disadvantaged to the national stage. The 1970s and 1980s saw black citizens run for the highest office in the land, producing an appreciation for political inclusiveness for black and minority groupings. Because of their aspirations, many others, including Al Sharpton, who took the Democratic presidential nominee stage in 2004, were able to articulate positions of importance to a national and specific demographic. Previous minority candidates, in terms of gender and race, allowed for Obama to claim a legitimate space on the stage for the visual expression of a black man articulating ideas for the future of the country. The civil rights giants of Jackson and Sharpton, both probably grossly underqualified in terms of national leadership, understood that their presence and ability to gain any small chunk of a voting bloc would be a victory for minority representation. Even if Obama merely had moved the agenda forward beyond the scope of what Jackson and Sharpton had done, it would still have been an undeniable and progressive step toward political equality for minorities. Instead, Obama's solid credentials, vision, timing, and multiracial heritage were enough to galvanize the masses in the idea that this change was necessary now.

Not only politically, but from a familial perspective, Obama is changing a long static dynamic of black manhood. Similar to the Huxtables, the doctor-husband/lawyer-wife couple of Bill Cosby's famous sitcom, *The Cosby Show*, there is now a freshness in the air, on a national and non-fiction level, that black families of this caliber really exist. Barack Obama, contradicting the absent black father image, took the real-life Cosby show across the country on the campaign trail to expose the normalcy of his family to mainstream white America. Obama's wife, Michelle, an equally intelligent, articulate legal mind, will make her own mark as the first black first lady, but make no mistake: the draw was the black man who professed a vision for changing the country. What is also interesting is that Obama seemingly plays a deferential role in speaking of his wife. One might observe this as uncustomary of the most powerful man in the country given the gender inequality that exists in society. One may also assume that presidential history would reveal a more subtle acknowledgment of a spouse's contribution and a direct allegiance to the script of the wise and fearless male leader. Obama's admiration, or reverence, of who she is as a person and his wife, may serve as useful symbolism for the powerful role that women have both as individuals and as primary supporters of their husband's ambitions.

This type of symbolism in the Obama era means that there is a new value standard emerging for leadership, for intellectualism, and for family. Prior to this moment, black males were not perceived to have a complete combination of these qualifications. Barack Obama helps to expand the notion that there are others outside of the traditional figures that society has grown accustomed to in leadership roles. In the key areas of manhood, Obama is perceivably executing on the highest level because, professionally, the presidency of the United States is the pinnacle of all leadership. Even children who wish to be doctors and lawyers when they get older have an understanding that the president has authority and responsibility for all Americans. For many, the president of the United States of America symbolizes the human closest to God himself. Now, although that may seem like a statement made in jest, one would acknowledge that the leadership of this nation, and the unspoken Christian religious morality associated with the office, is revered by most. And speaking symbolically again, this office has traditionally and functionally been the birthright of men of European descent. Young white males have grown up with the ultimate level of optimism because the imaging of leadership and morality has always reflected a familiar countenance. This thinking is seared so deep in the mind of Americans that the European image is even cast for the ubiquitous, all-knowing, and all-loving Jesus Christ. As of Obama's moment, this traditional symbolism of image for presidents has been deconstructed and the way we perceive this level of leadership will forever be changed.

Part of Obama's success has been a symbolic approach and philosophy that articulates abstract ideals that cause humans to seek their greatest good. His "mantra" of change was less about political operations and more about any American believing that they could be anything they desired to be. The paradigms are now being stretched, which allows for a variance of political, social, religious, economic, and demographic opinion. The "change" concept has spoken to those whose existence is now being validated through Obama, rhetorically, physically, and politically.

CONFLICT PERSPECTIVE

Due to the election of Barack Obama, there was a genuine excitement on the ground. Typically, "the ground" suggests the working class, the proletariat, and the disenfranchised masses who had a heartfelt desire for change. These folks, many young and not bound by the virulent history of American race relations, as well as those older, mature, and settled in their open-mindedness, decided to take the fate of the country in their hands. In Obama, the symbol of change, they saw someone who bridged the racial divides as well as the generational ones.

According to a general understanding of conflict theory, "social change is prompted primarily by economic influences" (Giddens et al. 2007:15). In this instance, the change appears to be less about economics and more about a holistic American ideal. In the case of the Obama victory, one could argue that an underclass rose up to challenge the ruling elite, whom they felt were disingenuous, politically visionless, and taking the country in a wrong direction. Conflict theorists believe that this is the type of direct action that is necessary to be taken if the working class is to assume its rightful place in society. This transition toward equality, as typically assumed, did not have to be bloody or violent. It was simply the united will of the disenfranchised citizens who took the abstract art of change and turned it into the concrete substance of action.

Karl Marx, the father of Marxism and conflict orientation, spoke of the urgency of such a time, although the vision may have been radically different. A progressive social agenda, such as that espoused by black Power advocates in the 1960s and 1970s, calls for the definitions of society to be changed in order for a new social reality to be constructed. These philosophers knew that society must be drastically recomposed, a development that would result in a conflict between those who had power and those who desired their equal share. As articulated earlier, power has been elusive for blacks and many minority groups simply because they have minimal ownership in entities that define reality. Again, the most important virtue in America is power. Giddens et al. (2007) asserts:

> By power is meant the capability of individuals or group to make their own interests count, even when others resist. Power sometimes involves the direct use of force but is almost always accompanied by the development of ideas (ideologies), which are used to justify the actions of the powerful. (P. 20)

It is not a new belief that power is seen as something that would never be given up freely and would have to be seized through direct action, confrontation, and aggression. Barack Obama acknowledges progressive ideology, but for the greater good of the country, he deferred to the higher callings of the Constitution to stir the political waters for authenticity. In a time when politicians have appeared morally debased, Obama exposed class conflict as something that should not divide but something that should bring citizens together under the umbrella of a common humanity.

Class conflicts based on superiority and inferiority complexes of the biological falsehood of race have dire social consequences. Race, for far too long, has constrained Americans by the visual indicators that come along with racial differences thus creating social stratification. Traditional Marxist ideology suggests that a conflict of citizens will ultimately result in a classless society. To date, there is no certainty that this will be the sum of revolutionary action; however, a classless society was Marx's ideal. In this particular instance of Obama's peaceful transition to power, the question lingered: Are we moving to a "race-less" society?

Lest we forget, there were nearly 60 million people who did not vote for President Obama. These citizens, the minority electorate in this instance, have run further from the center. Be it the cause of partisan politics, ideology, or the matter of which we speak, race, many Americans were completely disengaged from what Obama appeared to offer. It can be argued that many saw the status quo changing, a capitalist system in jeopardy, and the overall look of the country beginning to change. Even internationally, this change led to sentiments such as this one offered by Artur Gorsky, a Polish legislator: "This marks the end of the white man's civilization. America will soon pay a high price for this quirk of democracy" (Whitlock 2008). This profound statement speaks to the overwhelming assertion that power concedes nothing and there is great fear in the power dynamic broadening.

With this minority Commander-in-Chief elected to office, it is safe to assume that the larger majority of Americans were comfortable with America moving toward greater equality in regard to race. It is a fact that this great nation, born of immigrants, will continue to have an influx of diverse citizens. However, the renewed emphasis on humanity will make race and culture something to celebrate and not strictly define or compartmentalize for the use of power. In fact, Obama's rhetoric underscored a new goal of not seeing our individual colors but the power in our collective destiny.

SUMMARY

Based on the original premise of this essay, black Americans, although still comprising a smaller proportional representation of the national population, have taken one giant step toward equality in the person of Barack Obama. Ushered in by the next generation of Americans, that majority seem to be made up of those who are less focused on race and more desirous of an inclusive society. In a summative statement, Barack Obama's election to the Presidency was the grandest momentary validation of black humanity.

If we can reassess this analysis, we recognize that the functionalist operation, as it speaks to race relations in America, is fluid and possibly transforming. The subordination of racial minorities may no longer be status quo and their presence should be accounted for. An unnamed United States president once said, "The clothes of the boy no longer fit the man." This phrase speaks to the ever-changing nature of functionalist and constitutional thought in American society. As a symbol, Obama thrusts American power and race dynamics into the conversation; however, it is naive to believe that racism has run its course.

Ralph Ellison, author of the *Invisible Man*, wrote "I am a man of substance, of flesh and bone, fiber and liquids-and I might even be said to possess a mind. I am invisible, understand, simply because people refuse to see me" (Ellison 1952:3). In the moment, black men may no longer feel invisible when it comes to leadership. Qualified minorities may now be given a second look in all of their endeavors, as opposed to immediate regard for another white applicant. The campaign, the election, and work of Barack Obama will set a new bar for which all minorities have to aspire. Generations of ignorance, perspectives of racial inferiority, and Bell Curve theories are all now being questioned.

Conflict theorists view racial inequality as imbedded in the fabric of America. With that, it is understood that the masses' shift in choice toward pluralism guarantees no certainty in its future. Individuals on the ground must find a way to maintain the "new" status quo, or some other powerful new idea will lead to this group's future disenfranchisement. For the powerful and the powerless, racial discord and the inability to meet the philosophy of self-responsibility and the mantra of "pull yo' self up by your own bootstraps" are the conservative perspectives offered to address the minority inadequacies in society. Obama's rise, coming from a single-parent home, abandoned by his father, reaching an achieved, not *ascribed*, level of status, dislodges any elite perceptions of minority inadequacy and provides a new challenge of hard work and responsibility for the disadvantaged. For this moment of Obama's intellectual, multiracial, and charismatic *coup d' etat*, America will be forced to confront many misguided notions and ideas.

Although the functionalist and conflict approaches to society yield no definitive return or permanency, the perspective of interaction, visual symbolism, and the rhetorical themes of unification are the reasons why racial cooperation could begin to exist and have some lasting impact. The symbolism offered via the Obama presidency opens the door for a broader humanity that is now etched in the collective memory of Americans. The era of postmodernism has paused for the opportunity to examine society from its new lens. Because of the contact hypothesis, which states that "in cooperative circumstances, interracial contact between people of equal status will cause them to become less prejudiced and to abandon old stereotypes" (Schaefer 2010:246), amalgamation and a genuine pluralistic society will have an opportunity for growth.

It has been — and is still — my argument that Barack Obama will be remembered as a great and historic president. However, he is a politician who has had to work within certain parameters. Not discounting his political vision and competency, I believe that the sheer symbolism of his presence will be his most significant legacy, not his policies to improve America. He is the leader of the free world in its most trying times and his legislative accomplishments and overall leadership will be judged individually and subjectively. His greatest gift to America will be his multiracial heritage and guiding principles that have been forged from that mold. In his speech on race, Obama (2008) speaks to these assets:

> I have brothers, sisters, nieces, nephews, uncles and cousins, of every race and every hue, scattered across three continents, and for as long as I live, I will never forget that in no other country on Earth is my story even possible. It's a story that hasn't made me the most conventional candidate. But it is a story that has seared into my genetic makeup the idea that this nation is more than the sum of its parts - that out of many, we are truly one.

His unique background and his holistic American values were why he was elected to change America. But America can't depend on Obama to be the only change: a whole generation of people must continue to progress, as this is merely one man's representation of *e Pluribus Unum*. This must be America's change. For us to form a more perfect union, we must all realize that out of many, we are one.

Queens Broken underestimated STRO

ORANT undervalued RESILIENT Violent Marginalized CREATIVE Lazy

itual Dependent OPPRESSED Smart Confused Free athletic

ponsible LOUD Articulate THUG Brilliant inferior KING

ovative Artistic REGAL Queens Broken underestim

TRONG IGNORANT undervalued RESILIENT Violent Ma

ATIVE Lazy Conditioned Spiritual Dependent OPPRESSED Smart c

letic Stupid Irresponsible LOUD Articulate THUG Brillia

NGS slaves Innovative Artistic REGAL Queens Broke

derestimated STRONG IGNORANT undervalued

lent Marginalized CREATIVE Lazy Conditioned Spiritual Dependent

rt Confused Free athletic Stupid Irresponsible LOUD A

UG Brilliant inferior KINGS slaves Innovative Artistic REG

Queens Broken underestimated STRO

ORANT undervalued RESILIENT Violent Marginalized CREATIVE Lazy

itual Dependent OPPRESSED Smart Confused Free athletic

RAISING GIRLS

[INSIGHTS ON GENDER DIFFERENCE AND INEQUALITY]

To begin a conversation about sex and gender, I typically ask a class of students the question, "If you had a choice regarding the sex of your child, what would you have?" I quickly inform them that I am not interested in hearing the politically correct answer that one just wants the baby to be healthy. I want an honest preference. What would you say and why? The answers I hear and, more important, the reasons for those responses are interesting and varied.

I often ask myself, "If I had more children, would I want a girl or boy?" Having all daughters, one side of me, of course, says I would have a boy to have a different experience, greater balance in the house, and someone to carry on my name. He would be someone I could hang out with and just call "Buddy." On the other hand, having another girl would be a piece of cake. I've already done it…three times. I also know that there would be older sisters that could pass on hand-me downs, teach her how to go to the potty, and help with combing her hair. My leanings are clearly broken down along social support and financial lines.

The fact is that I have three, wonderful daughters. I've come to realize this was God's plan for me and I, in return, accept and love my role as their father. Equally or, possibly, more importantly, this role has forced me to examine how I view men and women in society. Understanding the patriarchal nature of American society (... and the world) — and the fact that masculinity is often more highly valued than things considered feminine — makes the task of raising girls harder than it may seem. Raising a young lady is a challenge due to the numerous mixed messages that society sends women daily about their value as human beings. However, with women always making new imprints on the American landscape, I am excited about supporting and sharing my daughters' aspirations and contributions, whatever they may be. As I think about their socialization and development, I plan to raise them in accordance with a few of the following insights.

SETTING THE FRAMEWORK

The reason I ask that initial question I mentioned earlier is to begin digging at notions of social privilege, in particular, the way we perceive sex and gender. What are the characteristics and behaviors that we are associating with a particular sex? What makes us think that that child would definitely be or carry out those particular characteristics? Before moving any further, let's clarify a few terms to make sure we are on the same page with regard to the topic.

In this essay, I will be using the word sex to describe anatomy and not an act. Sex is an individual's biological categorization as male or female. Gender is typically the cultural or social meaning of being (traditionally) male or female in a particular society. What is the difference between the two as they seem to say similar things? When we are talking about sex we are strictly talking about biology, one's physical or anatomical composition. Sex is biological while gender is a social construction. Gender is how we typically define one as a man or woman in terms of how they act, dress, etc. The problem is that defining individuals in this way lends itself to many different generalizations and stereotypes.

To illustrate the challenge of defining gender, let's look at a few traits and see if we can identify the gender associated with it. In other words, which terms are clearly identified as a feminine or masculine trait? Receptive? Cooperative? Dominant? Independent? Sexually aggressive? Sexual object? Weak? Intelligent? Competent or Incompetent? Rational or Irrational? Attractive because of physical appearance? As you read the characteristic, you get the feeling that some are specifically male or female, whereas some are less clear. In fact, this ambiguity is what gives fuel to transgender streams of thinking. If one cannot be definitively categorized to the exclusion of the other, can we even argue whether there are authentic gender differences? To this point, I offer a quote from an unknown source that reads, "You are born naked, the rest is drag." Without moving further on that notion, let's accept that gender lines may not be as clearly drawn as some make them seem.

Along with Schaefer (2010:280), most sociologists would agree that the functionalist approach to gender is that "gender differentiation contributes to social stability." Most of society believes that men and women have different and definitive characteristics. These two groups are thought to do different things based on their respective biology. Many of these behaviors are learned, with some possibly being instinctual, but society manages well when recognizing or clarifying these differences. There is the belief that complementing characteristics, a yin and yang, present a balance that is useful for the stability that society requires.

As well, the conflict perspective asserts that "gender inequality is rooted in the female-male power relationship" (Schaefer 2010:280). With that being said, the conflict perspective offers the idea that men and women are perceived as different and these differences create certain power dynamics. Gender inequality flourishes as certain superior or dominant characteristics are associated with one, while inadequacy and inferiority are attached to the other. Just as when we reviewed some of the "specific" gender traits of men and women, many of the characteristics that spoke to emotion and sensitivity were associated with women. Nearly all of the traits that spoke to power and aggression were associated with men. The belief that men are born powerful and that women are born with inferior capacities is the root of gender inequality in society.

Lastly, the interactionist perspective speaks to the way most people learn how men and women should act in society. As Schaefer (2010:80) points out, this theory asserts that "gender distinctions are reflected in people's everyday behavior" and people, predominantly children, learn through such observation. With the interactionist approach, we typically speak about gender differentiation described through the themes of "instrumentality" and "expressiveness." In relationships, there tends to be a kind of duality that exists. For example, in my home, if there is a hole in our roof or the car's tire goes flat, as the man, I feel it is my responsibility to get the matter resolved so that our lives continue uninterrupted. Conversely, expressiveness comes into play when my wife teaches or comforts our kids when there are life's lessons to be learned. She has greater patience and a nurturing spirit in this regard. Not that we are confined to these responses, but they just tend to be what we gravitate toward or feel is appropriate. In these instances, I can't say definitively whether her or my responses are learned or instinctual.

GENDER SOCIALIZATION

The challenges we have in trying definitively to categorize these attitudes and behaviors are what make it difficult to change these traits. The first fact is that gender socialization starts at birth. Let's recall what we've probably seen in the trajectory of our own lives. Once born, most all agree that baby boys get the blue outfits and baby girls get the pink outfits. The standard toys for boys are Legos, trucks, and footballs, while the girls have crafts, kitchen sets, and baby dolls. Boys are learning to build and exhibit physical dominance, whereas girls are being taught to communicate and take care of others. Children, at a young age, from the mere act of play, are being socialized into particular career pathways and taught to emphasize different strengths and capacities. As they matriculate through school, boys are treated differently in the classroom than girls are treated. Most often, girls excel in subjects requiring oral and written expression, while boys excel most when required to actively problem solve or perform on tasks where there are clear winners or losers. The young person's peer group or friendship circle affirms, by and large, that girls do certain things and boys do certain things. These expectations remain fairly consistent through teenage years, young adulthood, and oftentimes, transition into the work force. It will generally apply to their relationships, into marriage, and then they begin teaching these same behavioral expectations to their children. So, again, gender is learned … as well as instinctual.

JOB BY GENDER

If we carry this thinking into our professional lives, the characteristics will certainly yield specific placements for job seekers. Viewing a list of careers and professions in Lauer and Lauer's *Social Problems* (2013) textbook, women are merely 13.2% of civil engineers. However, women are 82% of elementary school teachers. Typically, librarians are positions held by women at a rate of 85%. Social workers are 81% female. Women dominate in front office or sales roles such as cashiers, secretaries, receptionists, and bank tellers. However, consider the occupation of fire-fighting where only 3.3% are women. Pest control, farming, fishing, and forestry workers have very few women employees. Carpenters, electricians, and highway maintenance workers continue the trend. Why do men and women have these respective jobs? What is it about women that may draw them to particular professions? Many would say they like helping people. Others would say they enjoy being expressive or creative. There are certainly many reasons to consider. I assert that these positions are channeled through socialization.

Many would argue that women are in particular professions because of something called the "glass ceiling." A glass ceiling is a term used to refer to the invisible barriers that limit a person's advancement. Essentially, the term describes the incidence of women, or certain disadvantaged groups, having pursued a position for advancement and finding that there is a barrier, unbeknownst to them, that will hinder their ascension. This barrier is typically a direct result of the hierarchy and norms within a particular industry and their decision to provide obstacles to a person's attempts for promotion.

A perfect example of nearly breaking through a glass ceiling was illustrated by Hillary Clinton. In 2008, once Clinton finally conceded that she had lost the Democratic nomination to then candidate Barack Obama, she made the profound statement in her speech that, "Although we weren't able to shatter that highest, hardest glass ceiling this time, thanks to you, it's got about 18 million cracks in it" (Clinton 2008). For those who are not overly familiar with these events, she was saying that through her campaign, and nearly becoming nominated as the first woman Democratic nominee for President, she and her supporters were able to shatter some major barriers for women. The people that voted for her and supported her campaign truly believed that a woman was capable of reaching the highest office in the land. So her statement that she cracked the glass ceiling was a gracious thank you to supporters and firm address to critics regarding people's beliefs in women leaders. Practically, as well as through her rhetoric, Clinton covered some serious ground in terms of women's advancement in politics.

In discussing gender and professional advancement, there is also another term to examine. The "glass escalator" is essentially the direct opposite of the glass ceiling. This concept suggests that when men are in occupations that are considered to be predominately female, they are pushed into positions of advancement much more rapidly than women. The field of nursing is a popular example. Usually male nurses or "murses," as they are known in some circles, are nudged toward medical school. It's socially presumed that "simply" caring for a patient is not enough: a man must solve the problem. Whether it's medical school, anesthesiology, or even nursing management, there is a perceived push for the male to pursue a higher level of leadership or authority. Similarly, this expectation exists within the field of teaching. If one has worked in or around education, it is understood that a male teacher is a prized commodity. However, oftentimes they don't last very long. Whether a physical education teacher or a chemistry teacher, many male instructors are pushed into positions of administration (e.g., vice principal, principal). The fact that there is inequality in regard to career upward mobility speaks to this glass escalator and the fact that men are typically advanced more quickly than their women counterparts.

GENDER INEQUALITY

Do these barriers have any validity? We must begin to answer the possible reasons why people are steered, perceivably by gender, into the various career fields. Sociologists label the process of qualifying male and female biological advantages as the "sociobiological perspective." This perspective asserts that men and women have anatomical strengths that suit their ability to do certain things well. One's capacity for tolerating danger and risk, as well as the use of strength and brawn, can lead to specific occupations. The degree of physicality of such work may determine the degree of compensation. As well, an aspect of Western society holds certain standards of what is considered beautiful. Women may often compare themselves against this standard of beauty, or "ideal," never fully reaching it. This type of thinking affects women not only socially and emotionally but often transcends into the workplace as well, limiting the type of work that they may consider ideal or appropriate. Consider these ideas in correlation with many female-dominated professions and we can give it the credibility it merits.

An interesting way of further examining the beauty myth is along cultural lines. If one looks at an image of a veiled woman, many Americans may see this as an oppressive aspect of a religion or Middle Eastern culture. Upon further study, we can learn that there are alternate ways of viewing the veil. In *Sociology*, Schaefer (2010:274) includes a caption next to an image that reads:

> This veil represents a rejection of the beauty myth which is so prevalent in western societies. While a Muslim woman's beauty is valued it is not to be seen or exploited or seen by the whole world. By covering themselves almost completely Muslims assure themselves and their families that their physical appearance will not play a role in their contexts outside the family. Rather these women will be known for their faith, intellect and their personalities.

This idea, on its face, through the Muslim eyes, is seen as something that is liberating because it's allowing the woman to be judged and valued for her humanity, for what she has to say, for her personality, and for her faith. This runs counter to the Western world's valuing a woman because she is voluptuous or her hair is flawless and all of those things that we have become accustomed to applauding. This is just an example of how this interactionist perspective manifests itself in various cultures.

When we discuss the traditional roles for married women and/or mothers, particularly those who are employed full-time, we must recognize the theory of the "second shift." This theory holds that just because you work during the day that doesn't mean that the work is over when you go home. The traditional homemaker role continues even if the woman is working forty hours per week outside of the home. There is still cooking to be done, cleaning, as well as managing the affairs of the home and children. To the contrary, since men are typically considered the providers or breadwinners, there is far greater leniency in terms of the expectations of what they are required to do once they get home. To the credit of the recent generation of husbands, this dynamic has been changing … and improving. However, I have heard many women jokingly, but seriously, state that "they need a wife," which speaks loudly to the frustration of the consummate free labor given by a wife to her family.

Whether learned or instinctual, I believe it is what I term *voluntary suppression* that denies at least half of women the capacity to pursue certain types of professional opportunities. So when we look at occupations such as secretaries, teachers, nurses, etc., a lot of those professions have greater leave flexibility and oftentimes are on a schedule during common business hours when children are typically in school. Employers will always be able to pay women less because these occupations typically aren't labor-intensive and don't call for long hours or risky assignments. As well, many employers are not going to pay top salaries to employees who may need to go out on maternity leave or may have to be available if a child gets sick at school. It would appear that the only solution to the professional inequity or lack of opportunity is for women to reconsider their role within their family. They cannot afford to wait for America to evolve into a more human-centered society that places a high priority on treating women and family fairly.

ONE'S OWN BIAS

To tease out any misconceptions as I present these notions and ideas to audiences, I begin by challenging women's biases about themselves. The point being is that if you, as a woman, can't get past certain "concrete" sexual or gender differences, then you can't expect the same from men who benefit from this patriarchal structure. Generally speaking, these biases are most prevalent in the areas of children and safety. Individuals must be forced to confront this thinking. I typically propose to audiences that they should not have any concerns with taking their children to a childcare service run by a man. This idea, to many men and women, is completely preposterous. The responses range from men's "innate inability" to nurture children all the way to their alleged, sexually aggressive behaviors. I release some tension in the room by admitting that I struggle with bias in some of these scenarios myself. But these are the ideas that we must confront and change if we want to challenge gender inequality.

An issue of safety arises again in the second scenario. I ask students to imagine your home being invaded in the middle of the night by burglars and you call 911 for assistance. As this scenario runs through your mind, I'm willing to bet that many envision, or are hoping for, a male police officer, not a woman, to provide the assistance. We can't deny these sociobiological differences, or beliefs, that arise and again taint our thinking regarding what is superior and what is inferior within a specific scenario. There is a certain amount of aggressiveness and strength that you presume that a male officer may have, which you may not associate with a female officer. The problem is that these biases push us down a path that is unfair and inconsistent, both personally and professionally.

If we deal with this topic honestly, some of us may also have to confront our faith. Religion is an area where gross inequality, visual and verbal, exists institutionally. An example of biblical scripture, Ephesians 5:22, asserts that "A woman should submit to her husband." Religious doctrine states that women need to acknowledge, listen to, and obey their husbands. Many rarely pay attention to the second portion of the verse, which says "a man should love his wife as Christ loved the church." That's an intense type of love. If he's doing that, then maybe he would deserve that type of submission. Unfortunately, that expectation or portion of the passage is seldom recognized by the man.

Moreover, institutionally, many churches are strictly patriarchal. I'd be curious to know how many people grew up with women pastors. Yes, the number is slowly growing; however, women in many places are not allowed into the pulpit as a primary pastor or official in church. There is a hierarchy in many different aspects of society that we casually ignore. If we are not paying attention to it, we are accepting it or even worse, contributing to it. Or, to go even further and because this requires such a major paradigm shift, many will struggle with this idea: Why is this force/spirit of God a man? Who has seen him to tell us this? Why can't God be a woman, or more appropriately, not assigned a gender at all? Keeping that in mind, are we now to assume that only men can be close to God since they are created in his likeness?

In regard to our acceptance of bias, the cliché adage remains true: "If we are not a part of the solution, we are part of the problem." The next question to grapple with is: Can men truly be part of the solution? Very similar to any efforts for freedom and equality, can the "oppressor" or privileged percentage be a part of the change? At what point does the support of this group become the center of the agenda and dialogue? Men must be challenged and willing to accept change, but women have to be the drivers of this vehicle for change.

VOLUNTARY SUPPRESSION

This movement must begin with a challenge, in fact, a confrontation of the status quo regarding marriage and family. These entities are at the epicenter of what many women consider sources of oppression. So, to a classroom of women I will often pose this scenario. Imagine that when you graduate from college, you immediately get offered the job of your dreams. In this scenario, you are also married with two young children. The caveat is that you need to travel three weekends per month with this job. As I mentioned, we are talking about a dream job scenario. As I unveil these details the expression on many of the women's faces is priceless. Excitement, contemplation, and frustration seem to be the common responses. Some say that they have to think about it, a small few say that they would definitely take it, but, overwhelmingly, most say that they would turn it down. The envelope is pushed even further by reminding the women that turned down the offer that this is their dream job and that they have a spouse at home. What is the problem? One woman summed it up best, "I'm not leaving my children alone with my husband!" This is what I mean when I assert that the issue of gender inequality is, in part, an issue of voluntary suppression.

Needless to say, every male student in the room accepted the job without hesitation. They seemed to give little regard to the impact of their absence on the family, but remained focused on what this opportunity meant for them professionally. Men aren't forced to question how to combine their career with a family. It encourages one to call into question the instrumental trait of a male as provider, and whether this is learned or instinctual. Equally, we have to consider whether women are more apprehensive about taking the position due to an innate nurturing connection to their children, the family, and the home or whether it is, as some would describe, learned servitude.

FEMINIST THOUGHT AND ACTIONS

As a father of three girls, I have to try and help my girls prepare for the present reality. One way to do so is to be a father who supports feminist thought. Now some feminists would say fighting oppression means abandoning or modifying the traditional American concept of family. Evidence of this idea is highlighted by the many great women powerbrokers in America. For instance, media celebrities or political titans such as Oprah Winfrey, Condoleezza Rice, and Queen Latifah come up in this type of discussion. Why might they be considered powerbrokers? Each one of these women is unmarried, has no kids, and has the freedom to pursue whatever type of professional advancement they desire. Consider the politico Hillary Rodham Clinton as a powerbroker as well. Clinton is married but her child is an adult therefore allowing her to chase any aspirations she has for herself. The same is true for First Lady Michelle Obama. Although married with two children, her education and experiences make her totally capable of handling new goals and ambitions. She has, however, made it publicly clear that, at this moment in time, her focus is her children first and professional responsibilities second. Through these examples, we're able to see that life without family responsibilities makes professional pursuits a tad easier. However, a woman making proactive and deliberate decisions about her priorities seems to be the first big step.

The complexity of such a decision is reflected in the ascension of former Alaska Governor Sarah Palin. By accepting the position as the 2008 Republican Vice-Presidential nominee, Palin came under great scrutiny in the media because she had five children at home. As an additional note, the youngest has Down Syndrome and much of the traditionalist mothering sentiment was: How can she seriously consider being second in command in the most powerful nation on earth and maintain her responsibilities to her family? Of course, many more progressive women saw this as a perfect opportunity to put on display the multi-faceted power and leadership of women. Ultimately, the Republicans lost and Palin discontinued her term as Alaska Governor to be at home with her family. This begs the question: Will a woman's instincts always be with the home? Or better yet, what if she would have had these instincts when she was elected to the office of the vice president? This scenario, played out on a national stage, affords us the opportunity to wrestle with these ideas surrounding female leadership.

Moving toward closure on the topic, due to generations of tradition and hierarchy, I recognize it will take years to overcome this level of inequality. Sexism is truly the worst "ism" of all the forms of inequality and subjugation. I am, however, encouraged that women are challenging this dynamic daily and that they come supported by males accepting a backseat at home or the job. As mentioned in the previous section, there are many women who are continuously pushing female leadership forward. In the 1970s, Gloria Steinem was one of these thinkers. A few of her quotes below demonstrate her offerings.

- "The first problem for all of us, men and women, is not to learn, but to unlearn."
- "The truth will set you free. But first, it will piss you off."
- "Power can be taken, but not given. The process of the taking is empowerment in itself."
- "We've begun to raise daughters more like sons... but few have the courage to raise our sons more like daughters."

With this topic, I chose to stay away from race in an effort to fully focus on patriarchy and inequality and its impact on women in society. However, in a work on culture, context, and social awareness, I would be remiss if I didn't mention the likes of Bell Hooks, Audre Lorde, Patricia Hill Collins and other black feminists who see feminism as equally sex- and race-centered. Hill Collins (2000) sees black women as doubly oppressed because they suffer as a black person as well as a woman. She writes in her book, *Black Feminist Thought*, a preface to speak to the full contextualization of a broader mission.

> While I am quite familiar with a range of historical and contemporary white feminist theorists and certainly value their contributions to our understanding of gender, this is not a book about what black women think of White feminist ideas or how black women's ideas compare with those of prominent White feminist theorists ... In this volume, by placing African-American women's ideas in the center of analysis, I not only privilege those ideas but encourage White feminists, African-American men, and all others to investigate the similarities and differences among their own standpoints and those of African-American women. (P. vii)

Business leaders are also pushing the agenda forward. The COO of Facebook, Sheryl Sandberg, wrote about women not being afraid to pursue all the opportunities available to them. She suggests that women take a seat at the head table and make themselves a part of the conversation of leaders. Her book, *Lean In* (2013), is about fulfilling career ambitions and building life around that career aspiration first, as opposed to the other way around. She asserts that while single and without children, women need to make professional decisions without undetermined family considerations in mind. Sandberg believes women need to abandon the myth that they can't have it all.

Sueli Carneiro (1995:17) simplifies, without minimizing or specifying, a poignant point regarding the reality of the task set before all women. She asserts that "we have more to do than just hope for a better future...What we have to do is to organize, and to never stop questioning. What we have to do, as always, is plenty of work." Carneiro's quote simply speaks to the underrepresented majority, determining their mission and working to fulfill their desire for equality in society. The status quo must be turned on its head, and I believe women can accomplish this goal as they are no stranger to hard work.

It is these types of insights contained in this essay that I will share with my daughters. They cannot be fearful of any current social restrictions and must leverage any intellectual, experiential, or gender-related advantages available to them. Having sons to carry on one's name is excellent for the sake of family lineage. However, being able to assist my daughters in changing societal dynamics regarding inequality is priceless.

Queens Broken underestimated STRO

RANT undervalued RESILIENT Violent Marginalized CREATIVE Lazy

itual Dependent OPPRESSED Smart Confused Free athletic

ponsible LOUD Articulate THUG Brilliant inferior KING

vative Artistic REGAL Queens Broken underestir

TRONG IGNORANT undervalued RESILIENT Violent Ma

ATIVE Lazy Conditioned Spiritual Dependent OPPRESSED Smart

etic Stupid Irresponsible LOUD Articulate THUG Brillia

NGS slaves Innovative Artistic REGAL Queens Broke

derestimated STRONG IGNORANT undervalued

lent Marginalized CREATIVE Lazy Conditioned Spiritual Dependen

rt Confused Free athletic Stupid Irresponsible LOUD

UG Brilliant inferior KINGS slaves Innovative Artistic REG

Queens Broken underestimated STRO

RANT undervalued RESILIENT Violent Marginalized CREATIVE Lazy

itual Dependent OPPRESSED Smart Confused Free athletic

REACHING BLACK BOYS

[REFLECTIONS ON RESEARCH AND
CULTURAL-EMOTIONAL CONSIDERATIONS]

Out of this entire compilation of essays, I want to say that this is the most important topic to me. I write that because my belief is that the problems and solutions of the black community come from black men. Black boys often begin their lives as the most misperceived individuals in society. By sheer race and gender they are born with an ascribed status whose burden is so heavy that many succumb to the struggle of carrying such a load. Through this work, I hope to be able to share the best ways to engage with and provide opportunities for instruction, training, and development of this group of youngsters.

To inject some contextual thinking into mainstream thought, I offer a two-part essay on this topic. Such attention is warranted simply due to the fact that if one were to examine a report card for black boys, or any type of measurement for academic, social, and personal wellness, the results would be jaw-dropping and depressing. Some would assert that the performance of this group, or lack thereof, is a matter of individual choice or insufficient self-responsibility. Others would argue that there are numerous societal barriers that contribute to black boys' lack of well-being or preparation for success. We, as a society, must honestly grapple with the best ways in which to address this elephant, or better yet, boogey man, in the room. As an educator, my mission in this moment is simply to highlight what I know, what I've experienced, and what may be considered successful approaches in maximizing the potential of black boys.

Opposed to starting from a blank slate, I chose to use a template as a springboard to examine these issues and their complexity. Nearly twenty years ago, I wrote a thesis as one phase of the process of completing a Master's degree in Education. The paper, entitled "Culturally Appropriate Strategies, Techniques, and Interventions for Counseling African-American Males" examined the numerous contextual angles that must be considered and explored while counseling and, in a broader sense, educating this population of students. At the time that I wrote the thesis, I was unsure whether these approaches were appropriate and proven or simply utopian theory. Based on my professional insights in education, I hope to be able to offer some clear ideas of what is practical and pragmatic, as well as what is still idealistic and abstract. In the end, I hope that these observations will yield some understanding of the various approaches and ways to effectively engage young men of color.

At the outset, I should also mention that for this essay I see the parallels between the roles of counselor/client and educator/student as so common that I take the liberty of using them interchangeably in this work. Both roles are instructional in nature, with one professional delivering content-directed lessons while the other fosters more indirect, or human-centered, support of one's growth and development. They each desire to provide assistance to an individual as he travels developmentally (academically and personally) from one point to the next. Both relationships are dependent on the intangibles of motivation, encouragement, and parental expectations. Lastly, both counselors and educators understand that no client or student is ever a blank slate, either emotionally or intellectually, and the development must initiate from that individual point of contact.

MAINSTREAM THOUGHT

The backdrop of this thesis is established with an explanation of what a mainstream education would entail. For this work, mainstream is defined as instruction or programming driven by the cultural ideals of the American majority. Immediately, the ideas put forth within this essay begin to consider the cultural inconsistencies that exist between various groups of people. An educational curriculum and approach that engages only one frame of reference can be considered problematic for the minorities of that particular society. Intentionally or unintentionally, the absence of minority contributions within American history and tradition serves to bolster the establishment and continuation of a predominately white power structure and status quo.

As it relates to cultural inconsistencies in education, one example that quickly comes to mind is the Scholastic Assessment Test. Commonly known as the SAT, it is a standard indicator for college admission and an easy target to examine for critique. In the 1930s, when this test was created, we can all guess that it was probably not normed with a cross-sampling of students. In fact, the creator of the assessment is known to have written extensively on the superiority of certain races, supporting the Eugenics movement with those ideas. With these thoughts in mind, it becomes clear why the test would intentionally ignore people from different racial groups, various social classes, as well as women and individuals from different parts of the nation.

In regards to assessing one's aptitude for higher education, the SAT was far from a fair and impartial testing tool. So, the follow-up question becomes:

If you don't have the advantage of certain racial and economic privilege, are you insufficiently prepared for college? The SAT is just one example of what is considered mainstream education, so it is no wonder that when black boys attempt to compete on this stage, many often find frustration and a feeling of being out of place. This generic backdrop provides the narrative for how in many educational settings black male students have been square pegs being forced into triangular holes. I would be rich if I had a dime for every black boy that I have heard state that they are poor test-takers. Have we ever considered that it may not be the student, but the test?

Even today, there are still numerous critics of this examination as an indicator of college success or academic worthiness. Rebecca Ruiz's review (2011) of Joseph Soares *SAT Wars: The Case for Test-Optional College Admissions* confirms the criticism:

> His work points to racial biases against minorities in the SAT verbal section and gender biases against females in the math section. Through his own essays in the book, as well as those of contributors, which he edited, Mr. Soares seeks to build a case against the SAT. He characterizes it as a test that tends to favor white, male, upper income students with the means to prepare for it. Chang Young Chung, a statistical programmer, and Thomas J. Espenshade, a sociology professor, both at Princeton University, co-authored one chapter in which they cite a study that examined national SAT data from the late 1990s. That study broke applicants into three socio-economic classes. They found that 29 percent of students from the highest social class scored above 1400 on the SAT, compared to 24 percent of middle class students and 14 percent of lower class students. Turning that pyramid on its head, the study found that

those students from lower social classes were more likely to have earned a top high school GPA.

Although academic and testing standards have changed and are hopefully aiming at becoming more culturally neutral, it's still disheartening to think that many black boys have been considered, and have considered themselves, inept as a result of poor performance on a culturally biased examination.

CODE-SWITCHING

For black male students who have encountered this bias in their academic environments, this feeling may be reflective of the concept of "double consciousness that black American educator and sociologist, W.E.B. Du Bois ([1903]1995) espoused some 100 plus years ago.

It is a peculiar sensation, this double-consciousness, this sense of always looking at one's self through the eyes of others, of measuring one's soul by the tape of a world that looks on in amused contempt and pity. One ever feels his two-ness — an American, a Negro; two souls, two thoughts, two unreconciled strivings; two warring ideals in one dark body, whose dogged strength alone keeps it from being torn asunder.

The history of the American Negro is the history of this strife — this longing to attain self-conscious manhood, to merge his double self into a better and truer self. In this merging he wishes neither of the older selves to be lost. He does not wish to Africanize America, for America has too much to teach the world and Africa. He wouldn't bleach his Negro blood in a flood of white Americanism, for he knows that Negro blood has a message for the world. He simply wishes to make it possible for a man to be both a

Negro and an American without being cursed and spit upon by his fellows, without having the doors of opportunity closed roughly in his face. (P. 45)

This ability to manipulate two different cultural contexts is not an innate skill … it most certainly has to be learned. This duality of thought is typically expressed in behavior known by experts as "code-switching." Per the Merriam-Webster dictionary (2013), code-switching is "switching from the linguistic system of one language or dialect to that of another." In short, this can be a changing of language patterns, but I would often extend it to behavioral patterns based on social crowd and environment. An inability to code-switch is typically perceived as a student's learning or behavioral problem and not reflected as an educator's inability to reach the student or insufficient cultural training.

Just as black boys have to be trained to code-switch for better application of socio-cultural navigation, non-black educators have to be cognizant of the values important to this group of learners. Becoming "hip" to the language of interaction is key to this group of learners and may require some level of self-disclosure. Whether proving oneself to be authentic or acting, rapport can be established through certain language and posturing. Curriculum on competencies that recognize cultural differences should be of the highest priority in every educational setting.

CULTURALLY COMPETENT EDUCATORS

This cross-cultural training for educators is imperative because there is nothing black boys are more wary of than a non-black person having a condescending approach. My thesis accesses the work of Derald Wing Sue, counseling professional and author of *Counseling the Culturally Different: Theory and Practice*. Sue (1981) speaks to such missteps writing that "Anyone who tries too hard to show that he understands blacks doesn't understand them at all." He asserts that a healthy respect of various cultural strengths and values lead to many opportunities for intellectual engagement. In other words, there has to be a bridge built between black minority values and mainstream American values if there is a sincere interest in reaching this group.

The thesis also considers the crucial fact that so few counselors or educators are black males. For example, and this speaks to a broader, nation-wide dilemma in education, in 2013 in the state of Maryland (per the Maryland Staffer Teaching Report), only 18.6% of educators were males. As could be expected, the percentage decreases in a conversation specifying whether these male instructors are minority or not. The figure appears to be around 3.7% for the state of Maryland's black male teachers. Being taught by someone who has no cultural or gender-specific connection to how one sees the world can be an obvious barrier to learning.

With such a limited number of males in education, it is easy to see how black boys may have as few as one, possibly two, male teachers throughout a series of several grade levels. Male-to-male interaction is critical, particularly at the onset of male adolescence. This is why coaches become such an important part of the equation in working with black boys in the areas of training, strategy, competition, camaraderie, goal-setting, and how to fairly process winning and losing. Participating on a team with a stern but supportive coach can build a lot of the character traits that are expected of young men. In this environment, there is an instinctual respect and admiration for those who have a perspective that comes from a context similar to one's own.

To address this professional gender and culture gap, a few colleges have initiated "Call Me Mister" programs on their campuses. This program is designed to encourage a more diverse pool of male college students into the field of education. The goal is not merely to attract, train, and guide high-quality, diverse, male college students into the field of teaching, but also to highlight the profession as valued and stable. The broader social discrepancy of professional prestige and monetary value is one of the biggest reasons why many men won't consider education as an option. Again, the national and societal devaluing of education is a much larger and concerning discussion. But, in short, due to the struggle to attend, pay for, and succeed in college, many black American men refuse to choose a profession where continued financial struggles in their career field would be the norm.

MISTRUST AND LOW EXPECTATIONS

Due to the aforementioned limited cultural competency of many educators, expectations can be low and trust challenging to establish. As a personal example, I can't begin to count the number of my peers who resented their school counselors after being told in high school (late 1980s/early 1990s) to pursue vocational trades or pathways that didn't include higher education. These peers — now many of whom are doctors, nurses, engineers, and other professionals — are some of the brightest thinkers and hardest workers I know. To know that they were encouraged to lower their expectations because of someone else's preconceived notion about their potential is disheartening.

Mistrust is clearly evident when there is no cultural connection. Based on the experiences and reflections of my peers, I agree with the assertion of that time that "black students view counselors as instruments of oppression and as stumbling blocks around which they must somehow maneuver if their ambitions and aspirations do not coincide with those their counselors consider appropriate for them" (Russell 1970). Many educators operate with a bias of low expectation, as opposed to a willingness to avail students of any variety of professional pursuits. For the record, it should be noted that many Bell Curve-type assumptions, prevalent at that time, suggested that blacks weren't prepared for the rigor of higher intellectual exercise. Professor Ivory Toldson of Howard University mentions that similar notions and resultant practices still exist in that "many statistics are myths and not only does the data make everyone around them lower their expectations, starting an ambition destroying self-fulfilling prophecy, but it makes the boys lower their expectations for themselves" (Chiles 2013:124). In 2015, at least in the arenas in which I have worked, the profession does appear to hold a more optimistic educator.

Throughout the thesis, I also highlighted empathy, congruence, and unconditional positive regard as some of the most important aspects of the counselor/educator's interpersonal relationship with the client/student. All three terms involve approaches that demand genuine respect and sensitivity to the feelings, thoughts, and experiences of the individual. Black male students are incredibly adept in determining what feels real and who is perceived as putting up a front or façade. As the kids say, it is always best to "keep it 100%," code for being genuinely honest. As mentioned earlier, however, sometimes that may require the sharing of one's own history, experiences, and vulnerabilities. In short, it means attempting to reveal a common humanity.

In the countless workshops and presentations for black boys that I have been a part of, I would estimate that over 75% of the predominately black American male educators started with a statement suggesting that they have been where the students are coming from. Although I get personally frustrated with this regurgitation of rhetoric, I understand the usefulness of this introduction. This approach is important as it seeks to tap into the same personal, community, and societal struggle as experienced by the student. It serves as a key part of social identification with the young black male. It breaks down the mistrust of difference and connects with the aspect of struggle, which is still very much a part of the black community's orientation. Boys listen when they know the speaker has a familiarity with their experience. It's all about trust. Whether it's where one grew up, what school one attended, or how bad or tough one's neighborhood was, these cultural linkages never fail to be stated ... and sometimes, overstated. In fact, in many adult-exclusive conversations, I have affluent black male colleagues who continuously reflect on their upbringing, all in an effort to feel or remain connected with some of this underserved identity. These educators understand that these boys don't care what the teacher knows, until they know that the teacher cares.

TRANSITIONING TO MANHOOD

Authority, trust, rapport, and modeling are all important during the teen phase of development for black boys. An absence of father figures or positive male models, as well as an inability to relate to others, leads to strained relationships with other males who display authority.

> It is not unusual, therefore, for black males to reach adolescence with a basic mistrust of their environment, doubts about their abilities, and confusion about their place in the social structure. This makes developing an identity during the crucial boyhood-to-manhood transition of the adolescent years extremely problematic. Compounding this problem is the social reality that black boys may have to engage in the process of identity formation with minimal or no positive adult male role modeling. (Lee 1992:8).

During this phase, many black students rebuff any beliefs that a great white father (male educator) is present to support them. In a world where all the representations of power (predominantly white Anglo-Saxon, Protestant males) appear similar, it is hard for many black students to accept this person as legitimately sincere in his support. However, those sincere and naturally authentic educators know how to crack the code and become, "Mr. So-and-So is cool for a white dude." This is the goal because, let's be honest, there is a broader power structure at play between black and white as well as men and boys. This unwritten, yet symbolically evident, aspect of society does not excuse itself from the school house. There is a social hierarchy that exists and black (and Hispanic) men are typically at the bottom while white men are at the top. Thus, to make a connection successful, non-black male educators and counselors will undoubtedly require various attempts at establishing genuine rapport.

Traditionally, men and boys, across racial lines, in general, are conditioned to guard their shortcomings and inhibitions. So, naturally, when these young men are expected to reveal their true selves, there can be a resistance to share. This shutdown can be the beginning of a student establishing power through silence. In the best practices for reaching black boys, my research touches on a very popular response of black male clients/students: an act called the "cool pose." Like the various other defense mechanisms that humans have, the cool pose or lack of expression, is a way of guarding one's self from compromising personal autonomy or displaying/acknowledging feelings of inferiority. This avoidance posturing allows the student to appear as if he has chosen not to do something as opposed to being perceived as one who doesn't understand how to do something.

This resistance is an avoidance response to the feeling that may occur from being relegated to an inferior status, as opposed to a respected human who needs/wants to learn. As a black male client or student, the last person he wants to hand his self-autonomy over to is a white person, who may have nothing but good intentions, yet represents much of the image he has been taught to be cautious of. Even as a young educator, I experienced this feeling as I leaned on the support of a white male administrator as I expressed frustration with a black cultural/community concern at a predominately white school. I felt vulnerable as a man as I disclosed my feelings about an issue that he in no way had the ability to solve. It was at that moment that I recognized the strain and tension of needing support but not being comfortable trusting the capability or resources that I had available to me.

COLOR BLIND APPROACH

My thesis also acknowledges some of the key errors that many non-black educators make when working with black students. The issue of color blindness is mentioned in Carolyn Block's (1981) work on culturally appropriate counseling techniques. In 1981, an attempt to be color blind was probably considered not possible when working with populations of color. Now, fast forward 30 plus years of multicultural training and exposure: one would think that many areas of our country have a growing commitment and focus to the ideals of diversity.

The impact of race, in many places, is not as institutionally stark as in the past so I believe, maybe naively, that more direct and productive conversations can be had about culture and education within the context of working to create a true merit-based society. When educators understand some of the differences between race and culture, it becomes easier to not repeat historical errors. Race is designed to divide, whereas cultures can be recognized for their positive or negative contributions to society. To that point, not every problem that a black child faces is a direct result of his or her race in an oppressive society.

Oftentimes, the challenges of poverty and lower economic social class (which disproportionately impact minority groups) are the starting points for addressing a student's need. Some students just happen to grow up in difficult and complex situations in which poor familial decision-making continually compound a student's issues. There are times when black students don't need racial or cultural empathy but simply a safe place to reflect on their circumstance and how to process it.

THE PLAN

As an educator, I have learned that kids learn best when there is a tangible plan in place for them. Growing up in compromised situations, many black boys respond best when they understand the ultimate objective of the work and relationships they are expected to establish. Even 20 years ago, I believed that reality therapy or outlined strategies or plans of action work best. When helping students deal with a problem or reach a goal, the idea of working through an issue, reviewing all of the options available to them, and then writing out a plan of action is an approach that is second to none.

One reason this method works is that many students need an opportunity to confront, in a rational way, whatever reality it is that they are facing. There are options for every circumstance and most children, boys in particular, need assistance in visualizing, organizing, and processing the experience and then determining what the possibilities are. As many boys happen to be visual learners, writing down the proposed plans allows them to analyze the pros and cons of each decision, the order of actions, a timeline for execution, as well as a chance to review the results. The reality approach is an across-the-board best practice for all groups of students.

The key to William Glasser's approach is highlighted below:

> Help them make specific, workable plans to reconnect with the people they need, and then follow through on what was planned by helping them evaluate their progress. Based on their experience, counsellors may suggest plans, but should not give the message that there is only one plan. A plan is always open to revision or rejection by the counselee. (The Glasser Institute 2013)

This thesis also looks at existentialism as an approach. Existenialism takes the form of a higher level of thinking about one's way forward in life. The direction and choices are individualized and self-directed, leaving every outcome the responsibility of the individual and not the environment or society. This is less evident on the secondary levels of education and moreso applicable for college-bound students. This approach allows for the fruition of monikers such as "I think; therefore I am" or one of my favorites, "A boy has dreams, but a man has plans." This approach is about taking responsibility of one's circumstance and destiny. The portion of the thesis regarding a sociotherapeutic approach speaks to the nature of how we must evaluate and perform this task of education and support. There are various elements of personal, social, educational, and career dynamics within each intervention. Having a broad generalist approach to the holistic treatment or support of a student is necessary in areas where students need more assistance. Oftentimes, it is a breakdown or revelation of the mainstream reality juxtaposed with the student's current social understanding that I, as an educator, have to articulate to the student and/or parent.

This research moves to a close in discussing the concept of hope as an intervention. Any counselor, and hopefully most educators, can provide some level of optimism to any student problem or concern. It can be difficult, and the research holds that religious sanctuary can be the last or only vehicle that can provide that consistent and constant inspiration. There are several religious stories that can be connected to trials and tribulations of humans, and more specifically, black or oppressed men. Hope has to be crafted into an ultimate awareness or optimism that is directly interlinked with one's conscience and ambitions. Do I agree with the abstract element of hope? Absolutely. The positive energy acquired through prayer and hope is essential to this developmental process. We have to believe that what is good and right will ultimately come to fruition and encourage our clients and students to feel the same. Plus, quite frankly, this may be the last best strategy you have when working with someone who seems to have the worst of society placed upon their shoulders.

In closing, Jawanza Kunjufu has done valuable research in the areas of the holistic training of black boys. His series of works speaks to many of these same helpful and harmful elements of educators that I have discussed. Kunjufu (1985:19) lists what he defines as challenges to youngsters in adolescence and teen years:

- a decline in parental involvement,
- an increase in peer pressure,
- a decline in nurturance,
- a decline in teacher expectations,
- a lack of understanding of learning styles, and
- a lack of male teachers.

Our analyses of this issue were conducted separately, and a generation apart, but it is evident that the factors that contribute to the decline in black boys' achievement are the same, then and now. These are the challenges. We must now act on the solutions.

Queens Broken underestimated STRO

RANT undervalued RESILIENT Violent Marginalized CREATIVE Lazy

tual Dependent OPPRESSED Smart Confused Free athletic

onsible LOUD Articulate THUG Brilliant inferior KING

ative Artistic REGAL Queens Broken underestin

TRONG IGNORANT undervalued RESILIENT Violent Ma

ATIVE Lazy Conditioned Spiritual Dependent OPPRESSED Smart C

tic Stupid Irresponsible LOUD Articulate THUG Brillia

NGS slaves Innovative Artistic REGAL Queens Broke

erestimated STRONG IGNORANT undervalued

ent Marginalized CREATIVE Lazy Conditioned Spiritual Dependent

rt Confused Free athletic Stupid Irresponsible LOUD A

UG Brilliant inferior KINGS slaves Innovative Artistic REG

Queens Broken underestimated STRO

RANT undervalued RESILIENT Violent Marginalized CREATIVE Lazy

tual Dependent OPPRESSED Smart Confused Free athletic

TEACHING BLACK BOYS

[LESSONS ON MENTORING AND TRAINING
THE BLACK MALE IDENTITY]

Let's talk about educating black boys. For educators, the primary goal is to expose them to useful content, thereby implicitly helping them grow into responsible and productive citizens. However, some of the world disdains everything black boys represent. As one article title reads, "Black men are the receptacle for which we place our fears." One could ask, how could you say such a thing? Well, let me ask you, "Are you afraid of black boys?" In order to begin, an honest answer is needed. If there was any pause or reservation, you now understand the premise from which we are working. Let's begin an honest discussion on the best ways to address the challenges.

We learned from the previous essay on black boys about some of the cultural and emotional challenges that have an impact on our work with young men. To review, some of those factors dealt with mainstream biases, cultural competencies, man-to-man interactions, trust and expectations, and planning/goal-setting. Using that information as a jumpstart, we can begin to look at the training that needs to take place to overcome these barriers. Some of these hurdles are incredibly high. Before moving forward with a prescription for best practices, let's confront two of the major challenges facing today's black boys: specifically, fatherless homes and living in working class poverty. *Ebony* magazine recently completed a series on the social dynamics impacting black boys speaking to these major concerns. "Although the presence of fathers can mitigate the low expectations, it's not something many black boys will have available to them; more than (68 to) 70 percent of black children are being raised in single parent households" (Chiles 2013:126).

An understanding of those numbers clearly indicates how devastating societal injustice coupled with poor or consequential decision-making can impact the next generation of young men. The biggest negative influence in the life of a black child, I believe, is a fatherless home. Not only do children want for parental supervision and training, fatherless homes also affect financial stability and emotional wellness. It is not fatal, per se, but the child misses out on half of his identity and support system. Knowing that single-parent mothers comprise the greatest percentage of folks living in poverty, the child faces the double burden of being fatherless and, more than likely, poor.

With all humans, many of our personal problems are self-inflicted. However, unlike other groups, there are many tragedies that have been heaped upon the black man that have unfairly crafted his profile. Any brainstorming session about societal descriptions of black men too often yield labels such as uneducated, unmotivated, hypersexual, and violent. This creates a broader stereotype that not only impacts male adults but is passed down to a generation of boys as an expectation or default setting. The *Ebony* article continues:

"The criminalization and demonization of black men has turned the black community against itself," [Michelle] Alexander writes in her book, "unraveling community and family relationships, decimating networks of mutual support, and intensifying the shame and self-hate experienced by the current pariah caste." (Chiles 2013:142)

Across the country, this image is not just societal but is consequently carried into the schoolhouse, creating what is being called a School-to-Prison pipeline for many young black boys. Based on the limited cultural capacity to understand these boys at times, we need to explore why schools typically confront minor infractions with the most strict, corrective practices in educational settings. This zero tolerance type of policy exacerbates simple infractions and increases conflicts with those in authority, leading to a variety of consequences such as detentions, suspensions, and expulsions. Repercussions such as these lead to black boys' being out of school thereby producing potential long-term consequences that could lead to their being unemployed, unskilled and court-involved, as well as displaying an attitude of resistance to authority/laws in general.

Even in the midst of dealing with the heavy bias of being fatherless, poverty-stricken, stereotyped, and in need of intensive corrective behavior, we still need to find a way to educate these young men. To begin, it's only fair that we recognize the cumulative impact of this profile and the resultant stress. In the human brain, a young brain, specifically, the area called the prefrontal cortex begins undeveloped. However, it is designed to mature over time and to govern reason and rational thought. As Paul Tough (2012) illustrates in *How Children Succeed*, the stress of poverty can be traumatic on the development of the brain.

Stress psychologists have found ... "The part of the brain most affected by early stress is the prefrontal cortex, which is critical in self-regulatory activities of all kinds, emotional and cognitive. As a result, children who grow up in stressful environments generally find it harder to concentrate, harder to sit still, harder to rebound from disappointments, and harder to follow directions. And that has a direct effect on their performance in school. When you're overwhelmed by uncontrollable impulses and distracted by negative feelings, it's hard to learn the alphabet." (P. 17)

Within any honest discussion of black boys, we must at least give them the benefit of the doubt in dealing with this potential trauma. This impact could easily lead to fatalistic thinking that specifically excludes academic and social development to simply developing a survival mentality. A quote in Kevin Powell's *Black Male Handbook* emphasizes this point. In a conversation with a young black man who was essentially asked what is needed to be successful, he responded, "We need life skills. There is nothing that is teaching us how to live. Everything is about surviving, or dying" (2008:xxii). We all can imagine that the ethos of surviving and achieving can feel miles apart.

In my professional career, I have helped and have witnessed students overcome these challenges. Sadly, I've also witnessed many fall through the very large cracks. I believe as Tough does, that "Kids aren't good or bad. Some kids have good habits and some kids have bad habits" (2012:94). My support and advocacy of disadvantaged black male students have often meant the world to them in terms of opportunity. Whether through information sharing or resource distribution, exposure to the unknown, a conversation with a trusted source for affirmation or questions, or by providing letters of reference, my professional support has been impactful for many of these students. Particularly, as a black male educator with an advanced degree and a 501c3 entity, I have been able to leverage change from an institutional capacity. This ability to construct more opportunities and ideal scenarios for individuals who may not have access to such linkages is key to meeting academic and vocational demands, simultaneously; it addresses intangible necessities such as belonging, esteem, self-esteem, and socioemotional skills and learning. I am most proud of these public school and nonprofit efforts.

WHO AND WHY?

Over the years I've witnessed many black boys struggle academically and behaviorally in a school setting. Tough mentions that there is a "cultural dominant code of behavior" that is typically observed by all. This ultimately suggests that mainstream standards should be adopted (or assimilated) and there is an assumption made that all children understand this. Well, whether it's language, dress, or behavior, black boys often either struggle or are reluctant to make the transition to a mainstream stage or way of thinking. This orientation can appear different from an Afrocentric orientation. So, instead of code-switching, I like to call it "sociocultural navigation" that needs to be taught to these boys. There is an Afrocentric cultural value to being authentic and "keeping it real." Is this innate to the black psyche? Or is it a refusal to adopt a status quo that supports their mistreatment? Some boys resist wanting to be perceived as speaking "Standard English" or behaving properly because they would be seen as "acting white" and compromising their authentic selves. This resistance to carefully navigate each environment, and still remain true to oneself, is a training piece in which many black boys aren't being afforded a lesson.

My thesis research spoke to irrational thinking (... and inadequate planning) and I, again, see this as part of the sociocultural navigation strategy. Restricted to certain physical spaces and environments, it is difficult to see beyond the dreams or realities of those with whom you frequently interact. When black boys think that the only way for them to have a career is through sports or entertainment, it is because they have not been exposed or been trained to navigate any other possibilities. They understand, in a limited and shortsighted way, what appears to be the pathway to a career in the two areas. However, the pathway toward a career in medicine, engineering, or law may be foreign to their understanding, due to the lack of exposure to those areas.

Where do they begin? The institutional constructs necessary to get there may be absent in their community and the opportunity to witness these professions in another environment may just not have been available to these students. This is the importance of educational and cultural enrichment programs such as my nonprofit, *HUE Initiatives' Young Man Camp* workshops, college tours, and career presentations offered by professional black men.

An attitude of style and representation is also important to black men and culturally transferred to black boys. In a society where they feel powerless, black boys recognize the power of their bodies and image. Let's consider the young men who wear their hats backwards, pants sagging, or new fads such as getting multiple tattoos on their arms, hands, or neck. In my estimation, this is their (only) response of power that allows them to challenge mainstream rules and values. Some see this as a deathblow to their mainstream vocational possibilities, but as a sense of self-pride, this is their freedom of expression and identity. They have no other means to display their resistance except through their bodies. This conversation could also address many black boys' desire for value that is demonstrated through material items such as their obsession with tennis shoes, jewelry, cars, and clothes. They misinterpret these items as symbols of real power, when in actuality they are only superficial representations of such. Furthermore, our materialistic culture, rap music culture in particular, validates this "surface worth," which has led to the profile or "manhood box" (tough, stylish, having women and money) by which many black boys feel they must define themselves.

A study of traditional African culture offers the observer a clearer understanding of black male self-expression. In his work, *Empowering Young Black Males*, Courtland Lee (1992) speaks in depth of this cultural trait:

> Five important dimensions characterize black expressiveness. Each of these contribute significantly to black mental health and psychosocial development. These dimensions represent a healthy fusion of the cognitive, affective, and behavioral aspects of personality. First, black expressiveness is characterized by a high degree of emotional energy exhibited in interpersonal interactions and behavior. Second, it is marked by a propensity among black people to exhibit real, honest, and authentic behavior in all human relationships. Third, style and flair are hallmarks of this phenomenon. This is often seen in the creative manner black people have found to put their personalities on display. Fourth, it is seen in the language and speech traditions of black people, which are direct, creative, and communicate both information and significant affect. Finally, it is characterized by expressive movement. This is an ability to integrate thought, feeling, and movement into a whole and respond to the environment in a spontaneous fashion. (P. 12)

Due to these unique cultural traditions that often contradict the mainstream, the private and public school system school of thought has struggled with the prospect of educating and keeping the attention of these particular students. To this point, academic success rates for black boys are abysmal and a concrete and comprehensive effort has yet to be implemented. John Jackson (2012) of the Schott Foundation, an organization focused on improving public school education, recognizes the current state of academic affairs and the work left to be done.

However, if we are to be totally honest, the necessary systemic reforms and investments to significantly improve black males' outcomes and to provide them with a fair and substantive opportunity to learn have come at a painstakingly slow pace or not at all. So much so that our failure to institutionalize the supports necessary to provide black males with a substantive opportunity for success has yielded a climate where academically only 10 percent of black males in the United States are deemed proficient in 8th grade reading, and only 52% are graduating from high school in a four-year period. Thus the penal institutions remain populated with too many black males and the classroom student rolls with too few. At this rate of progress, with no "large scale" systemic intervention, it would take another 50 years to close the graduation gap between black males and their White male counterparts.

The Schott Foundation has consistently noted that these unconscionable outcomes for these young boys and men are not reflective of their potential nor their abilities—but a direct result of denying them equitable supports and resources they need to be fully engaged and succeed. This is the opportunity gap that is the root of the achievement gap.

HOW?

Until larger society chooses to grapple seriously with the challenges in education and economics, private and nonprofit entities must continue to offer (their) expertise and experience toward the development of options and solutions. The primary objective in these efforts is to assist with the code-switching and sociocultural navigation needed for black boys to be successful in America. As mentioned earlier, HUE Initiatives (HUE) defines itself as a nonprofit organization that offers quality educational and cultural programming in underserved communities. Our experiences provide participants with a greater knowledge of self, cultural awareness, and opportunities for educational and career exploration.

We have a straightforward approach to our enrichment activities that does three things. In our activities, we *isolate* the boys by working with them in all-male environments. With no audience to "shine" or act-out for (i.e., particularly girls) our homogenous environment can promote "thinking for thinking's sake." With the ever-often matriarchal structure of family and education, boys, through our program, are forced to "cut the umbilical cord" and fend for themselves intellectually and emotionally. Secondly, we continually *promote competition and challenge*. In the adult world, men enjoy competition and challenge through playing and viewing sports, as well as throughout our regular tasks and responsibilities. Being confronted with scenarios and forced to strategize, compete, and deal with the rewards or consequences of winning and losing is a key part of developing into a man. Lastly, we *expose* students to new environments and ways of thinking. College campuses, museums, and various business entities are frequent stops on our excursions. We understand that verbal direction and instruction are only the beginning of learning. Seeing and doing something is what peaks one's curiosity and reinforces a given lesson.

As monthly, seasonal, and short-term experiences, our Young Man Camp (YMC) summer enrichment program and academic year workshops are effective for the execution of our objectives. In a public or private school, teens' relationships flourish through interaction. However, it's difficult for staffers to manage the structure or detail of an enrichment construct consistently, particularly with other graduation requirements and state and federally directed mandates. As a support structure, to date, HUE has proven to be a solid blend of exposure, enrichment, and consistency, with needed male bonding and interaction. Instructional engagement is alive and well in these program spaces, and boys are more than willing to play their active part when they see the adult men doing so. A perfect example is a recent bowling trip and set of team-building exercises where we had a number of lessons incorporated into the outing. Within the context of a friendly game, the teens, and adult males, were able to feel the pressure of competitive engagement, the pride of victory, or the acceptance of the consequences of losing.

In keeping with my vision of exposure through YMC activities, I look to individuals such as Jeffrey Canada of the Harlem Children's Zone and Steve Perry as admirable contemporaries and inspirations for what they have been able to achieve in education for minority students. Canada maintains high expectations for students and their parents, all while incorporating cutting edge instruction in a lower socioeconomic area. Perry is the principal and founder of Capital Preparatory Magnet School in Connecticut as well as noted CNN cable television education contributor. The show that he hosts on TV One, *Save Our Sons*, is the perfect example of the sociotherapeutic approach needed in urban communities. With each student, Perry's intervention always deals with the psychological and emotional baggage/struggle first and then moves into securing the young man with opportunities within the institutions of the community. In short, his goal is to provide personal strategies (promoting forgiveness, establishing expectations, or accepting responsibility) for change for a client as well as structural changes (change of setting, providing opportunities, harnessing resources, etc.). Whether this structural change means working out with local athletes, shadowing a local business owner, taking a job in a barber shop, or some other "support" the key is to put the young man in position to be trained into manhood.

Programs such as this across the country are useful to support this needed training in sociocultural navigation. We know what happens when these institutions don't exist in the community for these youngsters. The old adage, "An idle mind is the devil's workshop" will plague these underserved areas.

> Without the influence of strong neighborhood institutions such as churches, community centers, businesses and political organizations, illegal activity is allowed to flourish" and "When boys hit adolescence, they start to slip away from their mothers. Many of them rush into the streets' waiting arms (Chiles 2013:126).

This supports my contention that informal mentoring relationships are not enough. That is "just" love, friendship and casual advisement. A sociotherapeutic approach immerses the young man in an environment where sociocultural/environmental navigation will be seen as vital to one's future. Being exposed to real life work and experiences allows the boys to be trained to see the world as men. Although Perry's show has demonstrated that this can work, the fact of the matter is that the institutions in many urban communities are equally as fragile as the young men. With the many broken, or best case, fragile family situations that exist in these areas, the sociotherapeutic approach depends on stability of other institutions (religious, educational, governmental, business) to help serve as encouraging teachers and supports.

Another key aspect of the YMC model is the importance of group intervention. Group-centered counseling that reflects black American cultural values is often more appropriate than individual counseling for black American males. Shipp (1983) asserted that "the group approach is more compatible with Afrocentric values than are other counseling strategies." First, as a way of establishing a collective rapport and identity, there are benefits to this approach. I have been able to outline the cultural values relevant to that particular experience. It is essentially a return to the communal orientation of African/Afro-centered life. For instance, on the first day of the Young Man Camp, we watch a portion of the film *Roots*, which shows the collective process, initiation, and rites of passage that young Kunta Kinte had to go through in his transition from a boy to a man. We replicate some of these processes by doing various team-building exercises that focus on leadership and collaboration so the boys learn how to depend on each other from the onset of the experience.

Courtland Lee (1992) again elaborates on this approach from an Afrocentric perspective.

> The program is a developmental "rites of passage" experience that was developed within the context and spirit of a traditional African ritual known as manhood training, popularized by Alex Haley (1976) in his classic saga *Roots*. Haley describes how during this training, adolescent boys in traditional African societies were isolated from their families for an extended period of time and given rigorous physical and mental training considered important in the development of men. This training was conducted by men from the community and had as its purpose the development of the attitudes and skills necessary to assume the responsibilities associated with the masculine role. If a boy successfully completed this training, he was formally acknowledged as a man among his people and accorded the rights and responsibilities of a man. (P. 41)

Today, outside of biological and physical changes, there is no process that helps young black boys to determine when they are prepared for, or have made, the transition to manhood. Our programming provides the foundation for one's examination of this self-discovery and personal evolution. This process is a vital component in maximizing the learning experience for all. From the very first day, the young men understand what the camp is about and the expected outcome for the entire group. Individually, and as a group, the students buy into the identity of "thinking," which hopefully allows for a continued awareness or need/want to continue such services and programs for self-enlightenment. When training is processed as a group, synergy can be developed, learning feels less threatening to individuals, and it provides an overall feeling that there are others who have the same questions, fears, and experiences as they.

Typically housed in schoolhouses, libraries, churches, and on college campuses, another great thing about the YMC approach is that it has a level of formality that is still intellectual, yet it maintains a sense of the common community touch. Instead of turning to formal or professional organizations, and experts, black boys tend to keep their problems to themselves or to seek help from informal groups. Boys often have to be helped with the sociocultural navigation of other places and experiences and barbershops, street corners, basketball courts and churches are the places where they may feel most comfortable. A focus on integrating our work into familiar community spaces is part of the beauty of the Young Man Camp program.

The next to last practice of educating black boys is placing context on their individual struggles by thoroughly examining their historical and cultural plight. Crafted for group instruction, this type of psychotherapy, if you will, allows the students an opportunity to explore conflicts outside themselves. This review of the cultural and historical eras and events of their people helps them to understand their "real" history. This is one of the Young Man Camp's major curriculum objectives. For example, facilitating discussions about the "N-word," analyzing hip-hop music, or engaging in conversation about the legacy of black culture are important activities for boys to participate in to understand their identity. Boys have to be shown the past, present, and future meanings of their actions and behaviors. "Black clients need to learn how they became the way they are and how social and economic forces shaped their personalities, before they can explore and evaluate viable and realistic alternatives in the light of their personal strengths and weaknesses" (Majors and Nikelley 1983). This examination of history, followed up with the development of college and career planning, supports the academic-emotional understanding required for implementation of merit-based learning and the human capital theory. As one can imagine, this is a complex task for a youngster to do by himself.

Holistically, HUE desires to take students to this place of independent navigation and more importantly, self-consciousness. Psychologist Na'im Akbar (1991) recognizes this as well:

> Consciousness is awareness. What is awareness? Awareness is the ability to see accurately what is. Being able to see accurately means that one must be properly oriented in space, time, and person, which means that the prerequisite for consciousness is to have some accurate image of one's self and the world in which one finds himself. (P. 12)

We take students from where they are and nudge them along in the journey to manhood and overall academic and personal development. HUE Initiatives is making underground strides using an enrichment template geared toward supporting and training black boys. We understand the challenges. More importantly, we understand the consequences of inaction.

Queens Broke'n underestimated STRONG

RANT undervalued RESILIENT Violent Marginalized CREATIVE Lazy

tual Dependent OPPRESSED Smart Confused Free athletic

onsible LOUD Articulate THUG Brilliant inferior KING

ative Artistic REGAL Queens Broken underestin

TRONG IGNORANT undervalued RESILIENT Violent Ma

ATIVE Lazy Conditioned Spiritual Dependent OPPRESSED Smart C

etic Stupid Irresponsible LOUD Articulate THUG Brillia

NGS slaves Innovative Artistic REGAL Queens Broke

erestimated STRONG IGNORANT undervalued

lent Marginalized CREATIVE Lazy Conditioned Spiritual Dependen

rt Confused Free athletic Stupid Irresponsible LOUD A

UG Brilliant inferior KINGS slaves Innovative Artistic REG

Queens Broken underestimated STRO

ORANT undervalued RESILIENT Violent Marginalized CREATIVE Lazy

tual Dependent OPPRESSED Smart Confused Free athletic

CHANGING FAMILY

[IDEALS AND ISSUES FOR SOCIETY, IN PARTICULAR, BLACK COMMUNITY LIFE]

One of the things that typically come to mind when I think of "family" is half of society's generally pessimistic outlook on the institution of marriage. I mean really, have you ever heard anyone ask someone the question, "Are you *happily* married?" Why do you think people ask that? In my opinion, the question speaks to the dysfunctional approach that Americans employ to examine marriage and, for that matter, life. I say so because I am not certain that happiness can be the measure against which we gauge success or satisfaction in our lives. The popular notion seems to be that if two individuals love each other and decide to join together, an assumed utopia follows because "love" supposedly binds the two "through thick and through thin." The counter-question I often pose is: "On a day-to-day basis, are people happy individually?" The answer is probably, "No," for many more that would care to admit as much. Of course, no one is happy every day. And for married people with families, this fact is due in part to the marriage/family-related challenges they face day after day. Part of navigating these challenges successfully comes from having a realistic understanding of what marriage and family *are* and *are not*, as well accepting that every day will not be a happy one, and that some will be quite the opposite. Linking two individuals who are incapable of understanding and accepting such assigns them to a partnership in which happiness inevitably will not always exist *and* its absence will be perceived as a failure of the couple's union.

In grappling with this thinking, I have come to believe that a more appropriate way to assess one's relationship is focus less on how happy you are and more on the satisfaction you feel in working together to attain success in your marriage, family, and life overall. We commonly recognize satisfactory as relatively good, with the understanding of occasional ups and downs. See, I'm satisfied in marriage. I'm very content and most days I'm even happy. I'm not *always* happy with myself; therefore, I can't always be happy in my relationship. However, in working through the ups and downs of life, my spouse and I have learned how to have a successful relationship. With all that said, the concepts of satisfaction and success are heavily reliant on one's perspective.

If we really want to delve into the topic of relationships, marriage, and family, we have to begin by uncovering the basic concepts and functions that frame our thinking around these important institutions. When meeting my students at the start of a new semester, I typically ask them about their support systems and sources of motivation. Most cite their spouse parents, sibling(s), and/or a mentor. It's not until that question is posed that the students, it seems, begin to realize the value, trust, and faith that many have in this core group. If the institutions of marriage and family are to be sustained, then we must understand what we truly think about them in order to nurture and maintain them.

THE BASICS

I beg your indulgence as I approach this complex topic with the fluidity of expression it seems to require. Marriage and family are not exactly interchangeable terms, so I will be careful not to present them as such within this essay. However, the obvious correlation between the two and the fact that many may see them as very much the same, for all intents and purposes, may lead me to choose one term when either would do. I will leave the choice to the discretion of the reader.

From the outset, I'd like to make clear that I want to consider marriage and family in their broadest sense. People see family, for example, in many different ways; however, I think it's important to examine its traditional functions and responsibilities before we explore the modern family in terms of the challenges they face and solutions they've developed. Most sociologists would define a family as a group of people related by marriage, blood, or adoption, which serves as an economic unit, and is responsible for the socialization of the young. As a child, you learn early on whom you can depend on and trust in your family. The basic provisions of shelter and sustenance, a bed, a blanket, three meals per day, and person-to-person interaction are some of the essentials most of us will likely agree define the most basic of family functions. As well, education, including religious orientation and recreational activity, are examples of higher-level essentials involving the social functions of the family. So a family operating as described above, fulfilling these functions, is referred to as a "primary group." The primary group is composed of those individuals with whom we have intimate, face-to-face interaction on a consistent basis, such as parents, spouse, children, and close friends.

Family problems arise when the foundations of these alliances and supports are disrupted. An imbalance or inconsistency between the primary group and the functions that that group ordinarily executes leads to a high incidence of family dysfunction. In exploring dysfunction, we can talk about various forms of abuse or neglect, separation, and divorce (as well as remarriage and blended families) in that, all such situations can cause change and instability within one's existence — which, in turn, can lead to more troubling scenarios. Consider the frustration of instability and mistrust in marriage or the fact that nearly 30% of murders are committed against family members. Let me repeat that. For every four murders, one of them involves family-to-family violence (Lauer and Lauer 2013). We can also mull over the fact that one-third of American women will be raped or sexually coerced by a husband or partner (Lauer and Lauer 2013). Some might ask, even today, "Is it possible for a husband to rape his wife?" The startling variance in answers reflects the ambiguity that exists, *persists*, around our understandings of and expectations for marriage/family and its roles.

THE STRUCTURE

In order to continue to shape this essay of marriage and family, the broader, structural ideas associated with the topic should be explored. One of the first ideas to probe is the family's role as it contributes to the stability of society. Let's start with some general assumptions. The traditional family, or nuclear family, is the construct of two parents, historically man and woman, and their children (typically two or more), under one roof. Quite often there is a belief that more stability exists in that particular family makeup than in alternative structures. Every area of wellness for the members of that family, and more broadly, community, would suggest that this is true. In addition, higher income, community cohesion, safety, better education outcomes, etc., are all variables believed to be higher in communities with high percentages of nuclear families. One's family background, for better and for worse, gives us some understanding of how one may view and navigate in the world. The various types of family structures lead to varying types of cultural values that appear consistent within particular communities. From a functionalist perspective, on both local and national levels, it is clear that cohesive, family units provide a fair amount of individual and societal stability.

Because one does not select the family into which one is born, the family can perpetuate personal and/or generational inequality. Now this could manifest itself in a few different ways. When one thinks of inequality within a family, what comes to mind? One thought could be that of role differentiation and division of labor between a husband and wife, whereby the two have not only different, but unequal (in terms of perceived value, level of time/effort required, etc.), roles/duties within the family. An example is the concept of the "second shift." In today's society, with many families having both parents working, this term refers to the fact that the woman/wife/mother may work during the day and then come home and assume the lion's share of the work to be done at home — tasks such as cooking, cleaning, and taking care of the children. Even though research is beginning to indicate an increase in male participation in domestic activities, there is no denying the disproportion that exists for most women in terms of workload in the home. As a personal example, my kids will often walk right past me and go to my wife for assistance, even though I've told them I am also there to help. Now, for as long as we can remember, these are the optics of the roles that have been established in the traditional home. However, in a society that is producing an equal or, at least, growing number of women professionals, we have to consider whether the imbalance between men and women in terms of home workload is appropriate.

GENERATIONS

There's another type of conflict that comes to mind when we talk about inequality in the family. Examining all of the sociological theories regarding the *division of labor*, *organic solidarity*, *life chances*, *ascribed* versus *achieved status*, etc., it's easy to conclude that there are distinct advantages or disadvantages to being born into a given family. When considering the overall success of members in a well-functioning family in terms of a variety of indicators – such as quality of education, level of professional achievement, material wealth (real estate, investments), success of key relationships, and cohesiveness/effectiveness of networks – we see that wealth and privilege are obviously passed down from one generation to the next. On the other hand, in some families, disadvantages are passed down from generation to generation, including poverty, limited opportunity, and dysfunction. Whether assessed within the framework of socio-economic status, race, geographic location, there are certain advantages, plain and simple, to being born into a more affluent family. For example, I'll take a wild guess and bet that if you had grown up in either the Kennedy or the Hilton family, your life would be much different from how it is right now. You would have a different understanding of money, level of resources, access to opportunity, worldview, and perspective on life.

An example that highlights these differences in *life chances* occurred in the 2012 presidential debates. On a campaign stop, millionaire republican contender, Mitt Romney, gave some "encouraging" advice to students on how to be successful: "Take a risk, get the education, borrow money if you have to from your parents, start a business" (2012). Understanding that not everybody has that same opportunity to simply "borrow money ... from your parents," we can easily observe how much family resources matter in American society. Just as wealth can transcend generations, the transmission of poverty can span generations as well — which may be the main reason why slavery is such a contentious subject. Incredible as it may seem, there are still so many Americans who would appear to be completely oblivious to the beneficial generational impact slavery may have had for some groups versus the devastatingly negative impact it had for those who were oppressed.

And it's from these advantaged or disadvantaged contexts that people come to understand family and life. In observing the interaction among family members, individuals learn about the various roles and functions of family. Children and younger family members learn and confront gender roles, observing their elders in an attempt to understand how to live in society. So there are certain things that we may have seen our mothers or fathers do (or not do) that give us a perspective on how we should live our lives and guide our families. This perspective of observation is key to our individual and family interaction, identity, and vision.

REASONS FOR CHANGE AND FAILURE

Contemplating the tangible and intangible values of family, we see the logic of marriage being an ever-present staple of society. However, there is public acknowledgement confirming changes that run directly contrary to that notion. Much of this change may have to do with certain societal ideals about how we perceive freedom and our ability to change very impactful personal decisions.

To my knowledge, the only things required to get married are reaching a state-designated age and obtaining a marriage license. Religious institutions attempt to add another layer of legitimacy, as many churches will not marry a couple unless they go through counseling, which is absolutely a good thing. But, in terms of an actual policy or state or federal laws that outline specific criteria to be met or certain activities that must be completed beforehand, such as training or workshops, there aren't any. From a legal (as well as educational) standpoint, you have to jump through more hoops in order to be licensed to drive than to commit to a person for the rest of your life.

I guess this is where personal liberty and choice come in. You can consensually jeopardize your own existence (marriage) but it's not fair to jeopardize others' lives (driving). This thinking does make one wonder: Why does a society that supposedly values marriage make it so easy to marry and almost just as easy to get divorced? So when we talk about marriage in society, I believe it is the legal leniency that decreases the value of this particular institution.

HISTORICAL TRENDS AND REASONS FOR MARITAL FAILURE

Historically speaking, if we take a look at some of the changing percentages related to family, we will see some telling trends. In 1940, 84% of households included married couples — in 1960, 74%, in 1980, 61%, and in 2010, 50% (Schaefer 2010:308). Essentially, by the numbers, if you have a neighborhood of 100 homes, 50 of those homes will have married couples. The other 50 will be households either headed by a single parent or unmarried same-sex couples, or non-family households composed of people who are living alone or with other nonrelated singles, none of whom have children living with them. The tradition of the nuclear family as prominent is definitely changing. As a society, are there anticipated challenges to face by our moving away from a family rooted in marriage? My thinking is that the moral fabric of society will be impacted as the foundation that the institution of marriage provides becomes more and more fragile.

In lectures on family, I'll sometimes use texts such as *The 5 Love Languages: The Secret to Love that Lasts* (2015) by Gary Chapman. The reason why I like this resource is that it gives students a sense of what they truly desire in a relationship. The goal is to help people determine whether a potential partner is capable of meeting their needs and vice versa. There are certain behaviors that we all need in a mate/relationship and if you don't feel this person can give you what you need, then maybe you need to reconsider that relationship ... earlier rather than later. It often seems that the excitement of new love blurs the ability to see the short- or long-term realities. What I offer young people approaching marriage is a set of scenarios regarding their readiness to accept the unthinkable happening to their spouses (e.g., car accidents, cancer, and, ultimately, seeing their mate in a casket). People need to understand that one's spouse can be compromised in such a way that they never look, act, or even exist in the same manner as when they first got married. I emphasize the need to understand that this is a long-term proposition, that this is the person you are responsible for … literally "till death do you part." A major reason why the institution of marriage doesn't stay intact is that many people commit prematurely, without giving enough consideration to long-term possibilities and realities.

Another reason why marriage fails is because broader social norms have changed (Lauer and Lauer 2013). Divorce is widely accepted now. There's no shame in divorce anymore. Some would argue that this is a direct reflection of the self-ish and individualistic nature of our society. People in relationships could say, "I don't care if we have five kids or not. I'm out of here — I'm not happy." As we mentioned earlier, happiness and, its opposite, unhappiness are subjective, short-term emotions. For that reason, after the steady happiness that characterizes early relationships becomes less so and bouts of unhappiness creep in, a lot of people may abandon relationships, feeling it's perfectly acceptable. Many rationalize the relationship's termination by suggesting that it's okay to go your separate ways, simply as two individuals. I contend, however, that once you begin building a family together, parenting one or several children, then going your separate ways *should be* perceived as a little less acceptable.

Lauer and Lauer (2013) also suggest that role problems are having an impact on marriage sustainability. These are the gaps between your expectations of your mate's contribution to the relationship and their actual behavior. When one is about to enter into a marriage, there's often a thought that, "Oh, my spouse will now do this or that once we get married," or "Once we get married, it'll be great." And once there's this gap between the expectations and the actual behaviors, that's when problems begin for the relationship.

Lastly, one of the other reasons why marriage fails in present times is that children are often socialized with exposure to "bad" relationships (Lauer and Lauer 2013). Children observe many dysfunctional relationships and believe these instances to be the norm. And when parents walk out of a marriage or away from their family, children believe that abandoning a relationship/family is an acceptable/normal practice. Consider the messages that are sent when one has two parents, supposedly married, living in two separate houses. The overall message of such scenarios is that if you're not happy in a situation, then you are free to leave, having no commitment to stay. These types of breaks from what was the norm are what have altered the traditional structure of the institution of marriage.

THE BUSINESS OF MARRIAGE

For traditional marriage or the nuclear family to survive, American relationship and family constructs need to be reexamined. I assert that the goal of attaining individual and social stability has to be the focal point of the union. I will elaborate by returning to the subject of the unattainable ideal of consistently euphoric happiness in marriage. Already addressed are statistics demonstrating that throughout the last 60 years, divorce has been on the rise. I will highlight a few reasons that should shed some light on the explanations for this trend.

First, I believe folks need to understand and accept marriage as a "loving business venture." The goal, as I see it, is to choose someone you love, with whom you will *work* together to survive and thrive in the world. In other words, the goal is to be helpmates to one another. The concept of spouse as helper is illustrated throughout the Bible, but it is very simple and practical in day-to-day application. There are certain strengths and weaknesses that each mate may have; the goal is to balance out the strengths and weaknesses of your spouse — acting as a complement and support in some areas, taking the lead in others. When two people have children, the relationship takes on a new dimension. I consider it to be one of the family's greatest contributions to society when children are raised to be productive citizens. Breaking the original union between a husband and a wife makes this goal much more difficult.

Working from the perspective of marriage as a loving business venture, I often joke with others that I am going to arrange my kids' marriages. In this way, I can, to a degree, dictate their social status because they're going to be unhappy anyway ... they might as well marry well! I'm laughing as I type this, but, in all seriousness, if one thinks they are going to get "googly," heart-shaped eyes every time they see their mate, they may have another thing coming. I argue that in seeing your spouse, you will find your joy rooted more in simple companionship and knowing your mortgage and other bills are going to get paid, rather than in experiencing a romantic utopia. Unfortunately, for a successful long-term relationship, the desire for love and romance must be counterbalanced by the daily requirements of a sustainable existence. It's unrealistic to expect to feel the passionate love that you may have had during your first year of dating for the rest of your time together. Your love can actually increase, deepen, but that is often in the context of dealing with one another through all of the ups and downs that life has to offer. I think that, without recognizing it as such, a lot of people in successful marriages *do* look at it as a business relationship in that — although one loves their spouse, cares for them, and is attracted to them, most of their daily, ongoing sense of satisfaction and success as a couple comes from having learned to work well together.

BLACK AMERICAN PERSPECTIVE

As a black American, I am all the more sensitive to topics of marriage and family, as I comprehend their impact on upward mobility and cultural advancement, from an inter- and intra-generational perspective. I argue that the understanding of and commitment to these institutions (or lack thereof) constitute the single most important, defining factor in the instability existing within the black community today. The statistics on marriage from a racial angle suggest a number of sobering conclusions for this group. In examining the percentage of two-parent households per racial and ethnic groups (white, black, Hispanic, and Asian), every group is nearly 70% or above, with the exception of black Americans. Why and in what way is family instability so problematic for this particular racial group?

I assert that every aspect of a person's ascribed existence begins with their family. It is evident if we just pause and look at the socialization of children and the positive or deleterious effect of their family infrastructures. Is it merely coincidence that the greatest numbers of individuals who are in poverty were raised by single, minority mothers? With the previous factors and statistics in mind, we must also acknowledge that the criminal justice system is filled with individuals who come from the homes of broken families. So, as it relates to marriage, I ask: What is *not happening* in black American communities that *is happening* in white, Hispanic, Asian, or Pacific Islander communities? What is different? As Schaefer's (2010:315) figures indicate, only 32% of African American households are headed by two parents — why is that?

There are obviously a few hypotheses that could be considered about why the black family has been disproportionately affected by this blight. I won't write extensively on the matter here because there are enough assertions to complete another book; however, to acknowledge its significance and contextualize the matter, I must scratch the surface of a few ideas. The first thing we need to understand is that divorce, in itself, is not an overwhelming issue in the black community. The concern is that very few black folks are getting married relative to the numbers having children together. Unfortunately, the consequences are too severe for me to sugarcoat or coddle this topic. There are plenty of young black Americans who are unmarried and not quite "situated" in life yet have gone ahead with procreating. If anything is true that I have said thus far in this essay, then black Americans must take some level of responsibility for why they can't seem to climb out of this vicious cycle of poverty and consequently a lower quality of life — for themselves and their children.

My goal in this next section is not necessarily to answer all of the "why" questions, but set the template for a necessary and imminent discussion. Let's start from the early years of the black experience in America. One of the aspects of the slave experience is that these humans were brought from and sold to various people and plantations. These transactions not only occurred during the actual slave trade, but — in the Americas — could, based on a whim, dismantle and shatter any semblance of black family structure. A black man, for example, could exist on a plantation for years, be married to a fellow slave, have children with her, and then without warning that spouse, or the children, could be sold off to other plantations. In this tragic, frequently recurring scenario, it's certainly plausible that some level of familial apathy and emotional disengagement among the slaves would develop, even on an instinctual level — perhaps as a self-protective, survival measure. In addition, because of this known black experience, we can better understand how being received with open arms by the slaves on the new plantation may have created what we now view as the popular extended family structure. This experience allows for the joining of individuals merely in a capacity to survive, but not necessarily built with the same structure and certainty of an organic union. Could generations within this system of survival have permeated the psyche of blacks and created a broader and more fluid definition of family? I believe this is the case.

How could the internal frustration suffered by the male slave, the continuous feeling of powerlessness due to losing all he had in life (his wife and children, his role as protector and provider) — how could this *not* have an impact on his commitment to things that he wouldn't be allowed to maintain? The instinct to avoid experiences that are so fundamentally negating of one's self surely lies deep within us all. And what about the impact of slavery on the women? Certainly, we also must confront the psychological and physical violence of rape that many slave women suffered at the hands of the white slave masters. What types of attitudes, beliefs, and coping mechanisms would such horrific experiences instill in the black slave woman? They had to fight against or endure assault, while protecting those they birthed (often along with many whom they didn't), as they recognized all children as blameless in this great tragedy. Have these behaviors carried over into a "superwoman" mentality that still exists today? Is this the cause of the matriarchal instinct of the black woman, whereby she finds the means to protect and provide for herself and her children — with or without a man consistently in the picture? Were these behaviors reinforced through several generations, helping to establish the cyclical nature of the poor relationship exposure that we see today? These are all conceivable notions to consider.

Hundreds of years later, the government's safety net programs also put in place conditions that were not advantageous for helping struggling families stay together. During this era, in order for a low-income family to get any public assistance, there could be no working father/spouse in the home. Now this makes sense if the goal is to ensure that the system wasn't abused by a man simply not making as much as he would like and then collecting government funds. What took place, however, was that the government would offer more support, much more substantial than the father's low wages, if the father was not in the home. This created a situation that essentially provided an incentive for men to leave their homes. Because of discrimination and unfair working circumstances, many black men felt that if they couldn't work or make enough money to support their families, they would rather the mother get funds from the government to provide for herself and her children. The conclusion was that it'd be easier for the family to survive in this fashion, given that the man could, in theory, just fend for himself. The popular movie *Claudine* (1974), starring James Earl Jones and Diahann Carroll, portrays how these governmental and social processes unfolded. It is not a stretch to attribute these government qualifications as something that discouraged poor (black) families from staying together in an effort to survive.

Since the 1980s, many have attributed the "war on drugs" as a systematic governmental effort to remove black men from their homes and communities. If we consider the disparity in sentencing guidelines for certain types of drugs (those more common among blacks versus whites), we begin to understand the concept of differential justice. There are obvious, unjust terms of incarceration for infractions common in urban settings, thereby taking men from their families, leaving children without their fathers, all for their youngsters to possibly repeat the cycle. In other communities, certain drug arrests, particularly those for drugs associated with higher social status, such as powder cocaine, carry significantly less jail time (Alexander 2012). Not only is a prison sentence tough on a family, but also the reentry into society after a lengthy sentence is even more challenging for the individual, who now has a permanent status as a felon. I am in no way suggesting that criminal behavior not be addressed, only that it be addressed in a manner that is consistent. The disproportionate length of mandatory minimum sentencing guidelines for similar drugs and nonviolent offenses has a long-term cumulative impact on black men and consequently their families.

I wholeheartedly believe that each of these issues has led to some general deficiencies in the culture of marriage/family in the black community. Communities that are engineered to be matriarchal in structure will always fail in a patriarchal society. Of course, others may lean toward the idea that blacks willingly choose to participate in their own challenges by not seeking marriage or committing to other institutions. My unwavering position is that for generations, the exposure of "poor relationship culture" for blacks has led in a pathological way to an instinctual communal culture as it relates to family. This creates units in the community that don't have certain specific roles and the replication of these systems of survival creates a "Band-Aid" sort of support system but no infrastructure for which to build upon.

America as a whole can often be perceived as a selfish society and that's why marriage is declining and divorce is escalating across all groups. There is a public attitude of individualism that is natural to this society and its origins, which may also make one ponder the unanswerable question: "Are humans meant to be monogamous creatures?" It may be impossible to discern whether these issues point to legitimate underlying reasons or are to be regarded as excuses for the disproportionately high prevalence of single-parent families (whether through separation, divorce, never having married, etc.) among Americans. I believe, however, that it would greatly benefit the black community to pay particular attention to any challenges that may contribute to a pattern of deficiency in this area. If there is a continuation toward apathy in addressing these challenges, the impact will permanently cripple this community. I implore the black community to recognize and reckon with the adverse economic and identity travesty that is being created without this institutional staple.

CONSEQUENCES FOR BLACK CULTURE AND COMMUNITY

When sharing these positions with those who don't see the advantages of family constructs in modern society, I ask that they consider a few things. One, marriage is an institutional staple rooted in the fact that America is a capitalist country where certain ideals are beholden to success and security. Some would argue that, economically, marriage provides only a "few extra tax breaks & benefits." But, if true, we would have to ask the question, "Why do homosexual couples fight for the right to marry?" The reason is that aside from the wealth creation and family rights benefits bestowed upon the married, many of these individuals understand the psychosocial and even physical/health advantages of being in a recognized legal union.

Marriage is much more than joining together for financial gain (sharing expenses, often lowering taxes, building savings and other protections) or securing spousal rights, such as hospital visitation and survivor benefits. As discussed, many black Americans have been groomed to be shortsighted when it comes to the idea of generational wealth. Marriage makes it easier to attain home loans for building equity in a purchased property, as well as to get life insurance and pensions should your loved one expire. This is incredibly important. If my wife should expire, I would receive a more than adequate payout from life insurance to assist me with the children and other living expenses; and if I am the first to go, she would receive the same. When you don't have these securities in your relationship, you get nothing to help rebuild your life if the unthinkable occurs. These guarantees ensure a certain standard of living in your loved ones' existence in the present as well as after.

Another example in the cause advocating black Americans' reevaluation of marriage is the major economic differences that exist between whites and blacks in terms of homeownership. Being able to use your house as collateral is of the utmost importance in determining your assets and your liabilities. Historically, couples who weren't married rarely purchased property together, perhaps because there is no obvious or legally binding permanency to the relationship. And although there is an increase in unmarried couples becoming joint homeowners, information on how to avoid financial pitfalls if/when the relationship fails abounds, underscoring what we all know; many relationships don't last. Marriage, however, envelopes a couple in the idea of permanency and, thus, the willingness to invest and build together.

Black culture is fractured because not only is inadequate wealth creation taking place, the identity of future generations is tenuous. There is nothing that leads to a displaced identity more than when your momma's last name is Jones, your last name is Smith, and your brother's last name is Williams. Who the hell are you? What is it exactly that binds this family together? Without marriage, where is the historical or generational lineage that most use as an abstract or material foundation upon which to build? Black children don't deserve to be placed in such a precarious situation, starting life without the securities, assurances, and sense of belonging that all children need to thrive. Many families within the black community suffer because not only is wealth not being transferred, but also there is no cultural or family identity that is being transferred from generation to generation.

Many blacks have bought into a black superwoman theory, as previously described, that suggests that black women can adequately raise children on their own. Again, this is a trait that was forced upon black women, something that evolved as a means of surviving. Many in society have accepted this idea and in some cases perpetuated the thinking that a child support check makes up the difference for an absent father. This is absolutely false. The research on the positive social implications of two-parent households cannot be denied. From the areas of supervision, to education, to socialization and development of gender roles, to children less prone to juvenile delinquency, etc.; they are all improved in a two-parent household.

CLOSURE

So, where do we go from here? Marriage and "success" rates in society are powerfully correlated, in general, because when we talk about infrastructure, we clearly see that marriages and strong families create stability. I think we would all agree with the idea that a family headed by two caring adults is better equipped to function at peak performance. It's also easier to raise kids in this environment, with no one parent needing to be a "super parent" and this structure just doesn't exist in decent numbers for people who are black.

One's mindset changes when they pursue building a family, as opposed to when they're operating as a "single" individual. In fact, all of American society would do themselves a favor to revisit the pros and cons of this institution. I believe that communities across the nation could be changed or altered for the better, if individuals were married ... if families stayed together. Again, a critical reexamination and recommitment to marriage would be a pivotal solution to many of the social problems that black Americans face. There are historically learned, problematic behaviors and habits that have come to characterize the black familial experience, and these can no longer be overlooked or placed in another man's lap. It's not completely blacks' fault, but it's completely blacks' problem. Instead of conceding to individualism and the impact of the "changing family," people must be courageous enough to begin *changing* family.

Queens Broken underestimated STRO

RANT undervalued RESILIENT Violent Marginalized CREATIVE Lazy

tual Dependent OPPRESSED Smart Confused Free athletic

onsible LOUD Articulate THUG Brilliant inferior KING

vative Artistic REGAL Queens Broken underestin

TRONG IGNORANT undervalued RESILIENT Violent Ma

ATIVE Lazy Conditioned Spiritual Dependent OPPRESSED Smart C

tic Stupid Irresponsible LOUD Articulate THUG Brillia

NGS slaves Innovative Artistic REGAL Queens Broke

erestimated STRONG IGNORANT undervalued

lent Marginalized CREATIVE Lazy Conditioned Spiritual Dependent

rt Confused Free athletic Stupid Irresponsible LOUD A

UG Brilliant inferior KINGS slaves Innovative Artistic REG

Queens Broken underestimated STRO

RANT undervalued RESILIENT Violent Marginalized CREATIVE Lazy

tual Dependent OPPRESSED Smart Confused Free athletic

COMPLEX IDENTITY

[OPEN IDEAS ON BLACK SOLIDARITY AND THE LOVE OF MUSIC]

Every life has context and the simple facts are that many people don't appreciate the context of culture or recognize the privilege, or poison, ascribed to culture. Many of the foundational aspects of certain culture groups have been corrupted and compromised from the onset. Optics are important in this society and provide much nuance to the American experience. In this essay I will provide an opportunity for all individuals to see how this thing called culture has the ability to adequately define people, as well as to foster stereotypical misperceptions.

For black Americans, the collective building of a progressive, stable culture has been challenging, although some have been successful in accomplishing this in a localized manner, such as through family, academic, professional, religious, and social affiliations and organizations. The unanswered question has always been, "After being involuntarily moved to a new land, how does a group collectively establish a stable culture under constant suppression?" This is the 400-year-old predicament that no other group of people has had to entertain.

I find that the ability to understand a coerced removal and then forced new identity is best reflected in *Roots*, the 1977 TV miniseries. In the series, the strong and courageous slave Kunta Kinte, although captured, refused to be called by any other than his given African name. However, after the constant psychological brutality and numerous physical lashings in the new land, his body finally yielded to the weight of the oppression. In this particular scene, in the midst of being whipped, he was asked his name one last time. Kunta Kinte faintly uttered, "Toby," the name and identity being forced upon him by his oppressors. Although externally appearing to acquiesce, Kunta Kinte did not completely give up his identity, but instead learned to live in a state of "double-consciousness." This scenario provides the perfect narrative representation of the "current space," as well as subconscious resistance, of contemporary black Americans. Maintaining the last vestiges of one's cultural identity in the face of mainstream American norms and expectations is still a major tension for black Americans today.

THE BLACK UMBRELLA

The idea of a cultural identity comes with many question marks. One of the lingering issues of black life lies in the challenge of determining the "we" of black Americans. As with other racial/ethnic groups, blacks are not a monolithic body — although historically, by and large, blacks themselves and others see them as such. I offer this quote to define an often accurate depiction:

> "When it comes to doing something right, whites are a group and blacks are individuals. When it comes to doing something wrong, blacks are a group and whites are individuals." (Unknown)

This sentiment highlights the privilege of being able to separate oneself from the bad of society and the burden of always being attached to the worst of it. Why is this so? Let's take a look at the various aspects in defining the black umbrella. For years in my sociology classes, I have been able to initiate many stimulating conversations with my students who are classified under this umbrella. Often deliberately and intentionally, I will foster conversations that have foreign-born blacks (typically African or Caribbean) and multiracial students analyze "blackness" alongside American-born blacks. From an ethnocentric, outside-looking-in approach, other racial/ethnic groups may see these people as all the same. Internally, however, these groups see their differences as quite pronounced and as stark as day is to night.

During this session, we begin by completing a lesson called the Culture Tree. In this activity, we list aspects of our deep personal/racial culture (the tree roots) such as institutions and traditions for marriage, spirituality, the treatment of elders and children, as well as values and belief systems. We then examine our surface culture (the tree's branches and leaves), which includes the visual representations of a culture such as food, dress, music, dance, and other symbols. In this activity, the African-born blacks clearly perceive themselves as superior in culture to American-born blacks. In fact, I believe they would even question or generalize my identity had I not secured academic and cultural credentials by earning a Ph.D. and traveled to Africa for academic research and personal growth. Most of the African-born blacks see black American culture as diluted at best. The truth is that the interaction between these groups has been limited. And because of that, each group holds an unchallenged acceptance of many of the generalizations and stereotypes, as are held in mainstream society, of the other group.

Oftentimes, even as a member of black American society, I feel frustrated for my black American students, as the culture is perceived as shallow, volatile, "so impromptu," if you will — in contrast to the firm heritage in other parts of the melanin-filled world that has "better" endured the tragedies of racial oppression. My American-born black students obviously struggle to complete many aspects of the culture tree. Viewing this consistent occurrence through the lens of the "objective" instructor disheartens me. See, culture is learned through family, history, traditions, research, and experiences, as well as through immersion in other cultures. Unfortunately, many black Americans, gaining equality in stages, haven't been afforded and haven't created this type of sustainable cultural infrastructure.

One problem is that the American-born black cultural practices appear to be less innately developed, but created mostly in successive response to the oppression of early America. With that said, my lectures reveal the differences in culture-building that people haven't paid attention to. I love opening the eyes of the American-and, especially, foreign-born blacks to the convoluted story of black culture in this country. As the instructor, I must bring the students to an understanding of the nuances in the history of these various groups of people. We process each and every complicated aspect of the black umbrella.

Eugene Robinson's powerful book, *Disintegration* (2010), is a work I often use for a baseline reflection of the black umbrella. His book eloquently highlights four distinct groups of blacks and why the visual commonalities don't equate to agreed-upon, cultural universals. In American society, we have the lazy habit of believing that just because certain individuals may look similar to one another, they behave and see the world in exactly the same way. For all Americans, we must learn to take in the full breadth of one's experience to determine their humanity. Just to scratch the surface of this work, Robinson outlines the black umbrella in these few points.

Instead of one black America, now there are four:
- A *Mainstream middle-class majority* with a full ownership stake in American society.
- A *large, Abandoned minority* with less hope of escaping poverty and dysfunction than at any time since Reconstruction's crushing end.

- A *small Transcendent elite* with such enormous wealth, power, and influence that even white folks have to genuflect.
- Two *newly Emergent groups* who are individuals of mixed race heritage and communities of recent black immigrants-that make us wonder what "black" is even supposed to mean.

These four black Americas are increasingly distinct, separated by demography, geography, and psychology. They have different profiles, different mindsets, hopes, fears, and dreams. There are times and places where we all still come back together ... but more and more, however, we lead separate lives. (P. 5)

These groups are important to mention for three reasons as they speak to certain unspoken realities. One, in the early analysis (and engineering) of this society, racial eugenics advocates and other social architects pushed a notion that all folks were to be defined by color and blackness was meant to be placed at the bottom of the social hierarchy. Two, even when all the subgroups are combined, this black umbrella grouping is only 13% of America's population. As a legitimate minority group by number, there should be a focus and realistic analysis by blacks of how much power is reasonable to expect with that percentage. Lastly, these subgroups highlight other distinct schisms within the group, such as those who have a drop of black blood, those who immigrated from Africa, and those who are born here but have not seen, sought to know more about, or accepted their ancestral and cultural homeland — nor have any interest to do so. Understanding how these dynamics affect the subgroup as a whole is quite a chore as these groups are perceived as similar but are, in truth, worlds apart.

THE INTRICACIES OF SOLIDARITY

Woven within this seemingly monolithic identification is another complexity to living as a minority in American society: the understanding of monetary power and managing individual progress vs. collective growth. The fabric of America is undergirded by the economic system of capitalism. Simply put, this is the idea that ingenuity, innovation, and hard work will always be the tools that enable us to reach the dangling carrot of stability and prosperity. Consequently, this means that some people will often forego love and time with family and friends in a quest to reach the top of whatever personal or professional sector they desire to pursue. This response is no surprise as I believe certain elements of capitalism (which, in order to navigate successfully, may indeed require a degree of selfishness, are innate and that, by and large, we as humans will always seek our own self-interests first.

With that being said, traditionally, black societies have been perceived to be more human-centered in their worldviews. Although the consequences of individualism and capitalism are evident in various parts of Africa, traditionally, the deep or surface ethos of the continent has been communalist. Many people of African descent adopt an orientation that expresses that people are only people through others. Therefore, the understanding is that people must take care of one another.

On the surface, this orientation could appear quasi-socialist, but a better description might be humanist. In various aspects of African culture, there is the belief that there is always room for one more person. Although all American blacks are no longer in the same socioeconomic group, our pigmentation still has — by and large, as we learned in the previous section — the ability to define *and often unite* us as it did in the most tumultuous early years of this country. Referencing the quote from earlier, this is exactly why some blacks see themselves as a group often when something goes wrong ... or goes right. If we watch the news and a black person appears to have done something wrong, due to a common struggle, some black viewers may internalize the moment through kindred spirit. I'm not certain whether other minority racial groups feel this solidarity — this communalist feeling may be more innate rather than a learned behavior.

Conversations regarding this experiential solidarity have become more prevalent because of recent incidents in our country that have highlighted the troubled relationship between law enforcement and black men. This has led to many black men, from all walks of life, reflecting on negative encounters that they may have had in their lives with white male authority figures. While this feeling of solidarity is generally regarded as a positive force within a culture facing ongoing challenges, it can also — unfortunately — work against them as empathy creates a buffer or layer of protection, shielding people within that culture from "hearing" legitimate criticism of their missteps.

As cultural solidarity relates to financial success, to fully reap the benefits of capitalism, one has to be willing to leave some folks behind temporarily or, quite possibly, permanently. In order to be free and build wealth, one must be concerned with one's individual sustainability first and foremost. Some blacks, due to the history of collective struggle, continue to be limited in terms of the ability to pursue or achieve their own success; they may feel responsible for the whole race, attempting to bring all along in the process — an impossible feat. With that being said, others resist aspects of capitalism and the harsh realities of its zero-sum power approach, mindset, and behavior. The internal solidarity still lives on in many and there is a desire to stay connected to "the struggle." But, in America, you either have power or you don't. Unfortunately, to their own detriment, many blacks continue to subscribe to a (possibly inherent and instinctual) African-centered philosophy that is grounded in a communal idea of a collective humanity. This surely isn't always the case for the rest of the United States. A Western or Euro-centered approach may be more inclined to pursue individual success first, which, I agree, is appropriate for living in America. You will starve in the United States if you don't understand this system of thought.

But, let's make no mistakes; these individualistic values equally create success as well as problems in our society. My main point of contention is this "pull yourself up by your own bootstraps, even without owning boots" way of examining success, which is contradictory to the American ideals of democracy, equality, and most important freedom (... and Christianity too!). Freedom is completely different for someone who is poor than it is for someone well off. No one can argue against America's material wealth. It's the gap of unfulfilled promises of the formerly mentioned ideals and subsequent treatment of its people that many folks (nationally and internationally) loathe. In the end, we should not confuse a successful capitalist framework with the fulfillment of said humanist values that are espoused in the American constitution. Opportunities have been quite elusive for many because of the capitalist machine and "the -isms" (race, sex, class, etc.) that, arguably, are created to maintain it.

For black Americans, an identity rooted in collective struggle and resistance has been noble. However, when freedom has been granted by law, how does an identity of struggle/resistance transition to something even nobler? If your orientation is rooted in collective suffering, how do you then begin to progress to a mode of thinking or operating that allows for individual growth yet still fosters group representation and solidarity? If a cultural group does not harness and promote its collective strengths and gifts, mainstream society will establish cultural values on that group's behalf.

OPTICS AND PERCEPTION

One of my former professors at Howard University, Dr. Robert Cummings, would always say, "There is nothing more powerful than the power to define." What he meant by this was that if there is a blank canvas, it's easy for anyone to use it as the platform for whatever they desire to create. Once the optics have been created, the artist then controls what is or is not important about the creation based on their own definitions. In a certain sense, the black American cultural canvas, in an era of "freedom," has yet to be defined by blacks. What is represented on this canvas, however, is still, to a large degree, being decided by others for black Americans. The most lethal weapon — and a valuable tool — in this modern era of identity creation is the media.

The media has been the primary tool for shaping the images of American culture and, as part of that, black culture and social life. From family to business, art to politics, and everything in between, the media has a responsibility to educate, inform, and entertain its viewers. In just conceiving the content of this essay, we know it is a tall task to provide an unbiased look at cultural life without being immersed in that reality. We could look at media's role over time or we can focus on recent issues such as, in my opinion: some of the imbalanced analyses of black celebrity and sports figures; justice and community relations issues such as the Trayvon Martin, Mike Brown, and Eric Garner cases; and even the use of language such as "black-on-black crime" which creates unfair social narratives that have subconscious and real life consequences. However, as with everything else in this complex world, there are numerous points of view informing the media's interpretation of reality, so there must be some truth to it, right?

THE ALLURE OF MUSIC

In the context of any discussion of the media, the informative and yet ambiguous nature of its messages, I must speak my piece on the powerful impact of music in defining black culture. To speak directly to the point, I want to make the argument that corporate media forces, under the guise of free speech, are promoting a narrow cultural representation of black Americans to the world. More specifically,

I believe media gatekeepers have been/are negligent in their responsibility to limit much of rap music's negative content. Again, this stands as an issue that correlates mainstream norms of freedom with shallow black cultural standards that can allow the problem to be interpreted externally as well as internally.

Allow me to take a step back and completely contextualize my position. I'll begin with the idea that in Africa of old, the drum was a form of communication. From village to village, there were messages transmitted, ceremonies performed, and recreation enjoyed all to the sound of the drum. This musical and communicative medium is a part of black American social DNA that complements the cooperation and harmony of the communalist worldview. I also should mention that there is a spiritual aspect that correlates with the rhythm of ancestral music and an innate connection to love those things that touch the spirit.

If we examine this idea closer, we can easily reflect on how music has held a significant role in black life. Many historians note how, from the point of captivity, the drum and, more broadly, music became an extension of black life — as a tool of communication and recreation, or even for those planning a revolt. Starting with slavery, the musical and artistic solidarity of black Americans — as represented in the music of the Harlem Renaissance, protest songs of the Civil Rights era, modern day jazz, rhythm and blues, and hip-hop — has been an undeniable and necessary element of black culture. I argue that nothing, outside of religion, has been as important to this group as music because, through music, black Americans find freedom and strength, however transient, through the harmony of song, hand-clapping, and creation of sound. Throughout the black experience, music has been a lifeline for many, with every song and melody bringing reinvigorating precious and critical memories of persons, time, and space.

My position in this portion of the essay asserts that because of the obviously fragile infrastructure of black American society, the gatekeepers of music (recording companies, corporate entities, distributors, etc.) have been intentionally able to sabotage black culture. With the understanding that music means and has meant so much to various cultures and groups of people over time (e.g., self-expression, hope, salvation), it's my view that, in the name of capitalism, music is now being promoted to present itself as a self-inflicting weapon to the culture it purports to represent.

Here is how it is done. After reading psychologist Dr. Nelson Harrison's (2012) work on how hip-hop beats and violent lyrics hypnotize kids and change their behavior, I entertained a number of complementary thoughts as they ran through my mind. As important as music is to black folks, what if this dramatic poetry, this art that communicates the joys and frustrations of life, be given counter-productive lyrics? What if the provocative, compelling nature of the music keeps people tuned in, while the lyrics become ingrained as a result of the dedicated rhythm of the drum? As Harrison sees it:

> The drum machine was designed to imitate human drummers; however, the machine produces a quantized beat that is mathematically perfect. This makes it a perfect hypnotic trance inducer that allows post-hypnotic suggestions (the content) to become imbedded into the subconscious mind of the listener. The human subconscious mind receives its basic programming between the ages of zero to six years. We see the results of several decades of gangsta rap coming through the earphones worn by a child in diapers on a daily basis. It certainly is not the child's fault that their reality base consists of some of the images that the industry is putting in the market.

If this happens to be truth, consider the impact that music can have on a group of people who, again, may present in part as a blank canvas. If you are of African descent, consider your own responses to the drum. Have you ever been listening to a song with lyrics that are completely contrary to how you live and what you value/believe and you continue to listen anyway? Better yet, have you then turned the volume up and continued to bop (move) your head or tap your feet? This has happened to me more times than I can recall. Has one ever listened to gospel hip-hop and the response is the same, except there is a positive emotion in one's spirit? I believe that Harrison is onto something in his understanding of music and its trance-like impact on the brain. If you're still not convinced, ask yourself how you teach and how you first learned the alphabet — through a melody.

The reason that I pose the suggestion of a deliberate attempt to sabotage a culture is because rap music is such an easy target. If we consider jazz as an art form, the music is rhythmic but the lyrics aren't presented with the clarity of the poetry found in rap — they are more suggestive than definitive in terms of meaning. With jazz, the message is not as clear, as oftentimes there are no vocals to jazz music. How about we ponder rhythm and blues? The music is typically slow and steady, resonating with a gentler emotion within. With that pace, it's only natural that we are calmed and called to a more relaxed and reflective state, even when the lyrics reflect sorrow or injustice.

Now, let's deal with modern day rap music. As one who grew up on this music, I acknowledge a level of personal emotion in my position. I love this music, but it is creating and killing the culture it's supposed to reflect. In the late 1970s and 1980s, hip-hop began telling an authentic story of struggle, happiness, and cultural pride. Rap music, in my opinion the commercialized bastardization of hip-hop, represents the current subculture that has come to supplant, or occupy the open space in black institutional identity. The lyrics of violence, misogyny, crass materialism, and short-term decision-making are instilling dysfunctional values within a group of young people whose future will define in part the future of all Americans. One may ask, "But shouldn't parents be responsible for what kids listen to?" Others might ask, "Aren't the 'Parental Advisory: Explicit Lyrics' labels a good enough barometer by which parents can make decisions about what their child can listen to?" Both valid questions, but for me, this draws in a larger question of who allows music with vile language and destructive messages infiltrate the stores and airwaves? Does anyone even consider that the majority of "explicit lyric" labels are on music targeted to urban airwaves? Is this the only language that black artists/ listeners recognize? I don't think so. Even with "clean" versions, one can easily determine what offensive words have been bleeped out that their minds can easily reinsert them without wanting or intending to.

Before anyone suggests it, I'm not taking away any responsibility for these messages from the artists. They are sufficiently culpable. But, we have to be honest: what other American cultural groups have had 18- to 24-year-old men propped up to be the loudest voices of a cultural group? This dynamic appears to be intentionally orchestrated and, through these young voices, blackness is now reinforcing its status at the bottom of the social hierarchy. Men this age, of any group, don't have the social maturity to be the face and voice of that group. In turn, however, through the media, these images and messages translate into how American society and the rest of the world define black culture. The dilemma lies in giving poor and disadvantaged 20-year-old kids a microphone and money. At that age, what would *you* have talked about if provided such opportunity? This is a national problem.

I recognize that in a capitalist society, these young people are working and performing for fame as well as to put food on their tables. Our country practices freedom of speech and a musical career represents a legitimate opportunity to pursue one's livelihood/financial security. This is why the issue is so layered and complex.

So, I ask: Is this music really the artist's message? In my opinion, it is clear that the gatekeepers of media outlets only give broad exposure to certain music/artists. Urban stations are saturated with music that glorifies casual sex, violence, and other reckless behavior. I know the artistry is more diverse than what is played — and portrayed — in the mainstream urban markets. Let's experiment. Turn your radio to an urban station and determine for yourself if there is truth in my assertion.

To a degree, the future of black culture is now being controlled by "poets" who have at their disposal a microphone, a platform, and a hypnotic beat. Because of black Americans' sociohistorical connection to music, the drum especially, the population has an inability to resist the drum, making blacks easy victims to the deadly programming within the lyrics. No other culture or art form shares their truths to a melody. It can be debated, but this appears to be a deliberate strategy by media gatekeepers as rap is more ubiquitous than any other "art" form. The consequences of the majority of its messages will be fatally evident in this culture for the next generation.

Rap music has been called street poetry. In my opinion, poetry is not supposed to create culture, but simply reflect on it. Defenders of rap will state that all of the social ills portrayed in rap music lyrics existed before rap began to poeticize them. This is true. However, rap, as a business and professional pursuit, has offered many rap artists money, fame, and license to highlight these social ills as endemic only to urban communities. These stories have now become part of the written and recorded history of black life and identity and the positive or "socially conscious" hip-hop artists rarely have the financial backing or exposure to change or counter the narrative. As a so-called thinker, maybe I should try to put these words to a beat so individuals will be drawn to and begin to understand the truths that I am sharing.

The rap subculture is overpowering and supplanting an obviously weak black culture. Is the problem merely an issue of greater individual responsibility as it relates to freedom of speech? Or is this all in the interest of exploiting the challenges of a considerable portion of black America through *hypnotizing* the audience with these destructive lyrics? I think we all recognize the quandary and, in an era of an all-consuming and unchecked media presence, believe that we as a country have a duty to discuss the parameters of all media. The image and identity of black Americans, and all Americans, may never recover from the damage done through such dangerous programming.

As mentioned earlier, black life is quite nuanced and interwoven with issues that are, arguably, systematically calculated yet participant-supported. This conversation about the black umbrella, economic and philosophical solidarity, and black Americans' relationship with music is just the beginning of understanding some of this community's unique challenges. Image and identity drive perceptions of self and provide a lens through which others will view and often prejudge. These issues often appear quiet and unassuming and then grow into raging monsters. They are complex because of the difficulty in determining their origin and intention. I am bringing them to this audience so that we have alternative starting points from which to examine black culture and its relationship to American systems of influence, power, and inequality. Let's continue to talk.

Queens **Broken** underestimated STRO

RANT undervalued RESILIENT Violent Marginalized CREATIVE Lazy

tual Dependent OPPRESSED Smart Confused Free athletic

onsible LOUD Articulate THUG Brilliant inferior KING

vative Artistic REGAL Queens **Broken** underestin

TRONG IGNORANT undervalued RESILIENT Violent Ma

ATIVE Lazy Conditioned Spiritual Dependent OPPRESSED Smart

tic Stupid Irresponsible LOUD Articulate THUG Brillia

NGS slaves Innovative Artistic REGAL Queens **Broke**

erestimated STRONG IGNORANT undervalued

lent Marginalized CREATIVE Lazy Conditioned Spiritual Dependent

rt Confused Free athletic Stupid Irresponsible LOUD A

UG Brilliant inferior KINGS slaves Innovative Artistic REG

Queens **Broken** underestimated STRO

RANT undervalued RESILIENT Violent Marginalized CREATIVE Lazy

tual Dependent OPPRESSED Smart Confused Free athletic

CLOSING THOUGHTS
[CULTURAL CONSCIOUSNESS FOR ALL]

This, my friends, is the end of these important observations about the complexity of black culture and American social life. Depending on the reader, I'm sure these insights will be received as absolute truth, legitimate considerations, or exaggerated notions. Again, my main idea within this work was to give all people a few reference points from which to comprehend various aspects of the black experience. I wrote this because our children's children need us to not make the same assumptions and, consequently, mistakes of previous generations. It is indeed a tall task for us to critique and rethink some of these social norms and processes.

Cultural awareness has eluded nearly all of us. Most recognize that black Americans have come from a place of struggle and resistance and for the most part have learned to adapt and maintain. But, as discussed earlier, this shared history has engendered identity traits that are in fact strengths to be proud of, even though they have not yet led to the formation of a sustainable cultural infrastructure. I believe many would agree that adaptation could alternately be understood as creativity — that is, making unique changes in order to thrive in a particular context, oftentimes, whereby, something new and valuable is brought into existence. If you observe black folks, there is typically no shortage of creativity that is reflected in some of their language, family patterns, dress, food, and music, as well as nuances of their behaviors. The culture essentially has been developed *through* "adaptive creativity." As a norm, mainstream America typically doesn't care to discuss the cause and consequence of this identity.

In the late 1980s there was a popular slogan that many black folks used. The slogan, "It's a black thing, you wouldn't understand," essentially highlighted the fact that other races/cultures, looking from the outside, had no idea what a given thing ("the black thing") meant to the black American identity. It takes a lot of empathy and sociological imagination to care enough to reflect upon and realize how blacks have created everything they have from nothing. They've created music without instruments, just a handclap, toe-tap, and finger-snap. Young men on street corners have produced melodies with nothing more than buckets and different vocal sounds, such as improvised scats or beatboxing. There is individual creativity in every dance step, sneaker style, haircut, and variation on the use of Standard English or in celebration of the Creator. I see this all of this creativity as an attempt to resist full American assimilation, yet develop and produce something of unique value in the United States. In the worst of our history, slaves were given the scraps of the landowner and black families created quite tasty entrees out of these scraps, such as scrapple, pig's feet, hog maws, and chitterlings. From a health standpoint, has it been good to us? No. But life is not all about survival, not merely adopting a healthy or long-term mentality and physical practices, but often more of a short-term exercise in adaptive creativity.

I wrote these observations not as an appeal to mainstream society's moral consciousness but really as a simple statement of the complexity of black culture. There are many who needed to be offered a glimpse of the consequences of socialization under the veil of racial (and gender) bias and prejudice. In our society, some of the systems of suppression are so pervasive that they have simply become invisible. Blacks who call attention to these "invisible" barriers have been criticized for "playing the race card" and challenged to simply move on with their lives. Well, pardon me, but these types of insensitive directives would never be made to the victims of sexual abuse or post-traumatic stress from war without the required therapy and resources to address the causes underlying the issues. The cumulative impact of black trauma has taken a devastating cultural, psychological, and economic toll on a people, all while others remain — or pretend to be — unaware of the privilege of the advantages bestowed upon them by their forefathers' systematic misdeeds.

I am still in awe at those who are afraid to even talk about race relations and power dynamics in American society. My senses tell me avoidance of honest conversations exists because acknowledgment and redress would ultimately need to follow. And, the belief that blacks unnecessarily bring up the "race card" is silly when their identity has been created and formed under the duress of this very construct. Why wouldn't blacks, matter of fact, all Americans, understand that much of our social life is based on race? It is a true testament to our national immaturity that we can't have a more honest conversation. In fact, it seems foolish that as recently as a few years ago, people even hinted that we were in a post-racial society. As many of us are aware, the election of the first black president didn't eliminate racial tensions but instead has made us even more cognizant of the issues we have with race, power, and maintenance of a status quo.

Even without ever receiving amends, I begin to ask the black community what their responsibility is in terms of moving forward. Should black Americans seek recompense or just forgive and move toward a more sustainable culture, accepting the height of the mountain that they still have to climb? Are blacks better off with full assimilation into American ideals, given the opportunities that do exist in the United States? These race questions are manifestations of their *complex* and a resultant source of resentment that some blacks feel for America. It's the reason why 40 acres, a mule, and reparations would have mattered. It's the reason why some blacks mumble when they pledge to this flag of unrealized ideals. It's the reason why a government-issued apology could have begun to close an open wound. Nevertheless, as for progress, many blacks feel cautiously optimistic as education and hard work, along with the support of various hues of people, led to a bi-racial man and his black wife winning and occupying the White House … twice. Opportunities for success, although far too few, really can lie right around the corner and this is what drives people to risk their lives to be here.

See, America is what America has created. Whether one take that as good or bad may give you a suggestion of one's placement in society. The good thing is that there is still time and space for this country to grow. For black Americans, all Americans, the answers to the questions of race, culture, and inequality are as complex as they are simple. With works such as this, the complexity, misunderstandings, and labels are given more context for a better understanding of a people. The way forward doesn't exist without meeting and engaging one another as humans. This is the only way to begin to understand why black folks do what they do and why blackness is what it is. America is a land of beautiful hues and blackness isn't going anywhere. There is still a lot of work to be done to fully accept and appreciate its unique existence.

Queens Broken underestimated STRONG

RANT undervalued RESILIENT Violent Marginalized CREATIVE Lazy

tual Dependent OPPRESSED Smart Confused Free athletic

onsible LOUD Articulate THUG Brilliant inferior KINGS

ative Artistic REGAL Queens Broken underestin

TRONG IGNORANT undervalued RESILIENT Violent Ma

ATIVE Lazy Conditioned Spiritual Dependent OPPRESSED Smart C

atic Stupid Irresponsible LOUD Articulate THUG Brillia

NGS slaves Innovative Artistic REGAL Queens Brok

erestimated STRONG IGNORANT undervalued

lent Marginalized CREATIVE Lazy Conditioned Spiritual Dependent

rt Confused Free athletic Stupid Irresponsible LOUD A

UG Brilliant inferior KINGS slaves Innovative Artistic REG

Queens Broken underestimated STRO

RANT undervalued RESILIENT Violent Marginalized CREATIVE Lazy

tual Dependent OPPRESSED Smart Confused Free athletic

REFERENCES

Adelman, Larry et al. 2003. *Race: The Power of an Illusion*. DVD.
San Francisco: California Newsreel.

Akbar, Na'im. 1991. *Visions for Black Men*. Nashville, Tennessee:
Winston Derek Publishers.

Alexander, Michelle. 2012. *The New Jim Crow: Mass Incarceration in the Age of
Colorblindness*. New York: The New Press.

Berry, John. 1974. *Claudine*. Los Angeles, CA: Twentieth Century Fox.

Block, Carolyn B. 1981. "Black Americans and the Cross-Cultural Counseling
and Psychotherapy Experience." In A. Marsella and P. Person (Eds.),
Cross-Cultural Counseling and Psychotherapy (pp. 177-194). New York:
Pergamon Press.

Buchanan, Patrick. 2006. *State of Emergency: The Third World Invasion and Conquest of America.* New York: Thomas Dunne Books.

Carneiro, Sueli.1995. "Defining Black Feminism." In Achola O. Pala (Ed.) *Connecting Across Cultures and Continents; Black Women Speak Out on Identity, Race and Development* (pp. 11-18). New York: United Nations Development Fund for Women.

Chapman, Gary. 2015. *The 5 Love Languages: The Secret to Love that Lasts.* Chicago, IL: Northfield Publishing Company.

Chiles, Nick. 2013. "The State of Black Boys." *Ebony Magazine*, May 2013 (pp.122-127, 142).

Chomsky, Marvin et al. 1977. *Roots.* DVD. USA: Warner Home Video.

Clinton, Hillary. 2008. Speech. Presented at National Building Museum, June 7, Washington, D.C.

Code-switching. 2013. In *Merriam-Webster.com*. Retrieved May 8, 2013 (http://www.merriam-webster.com/dictionary).

Du Bois, W.E.B. [1903] 1995. *The Souls of Black Folk.* New York: Signet Classic.

Ellison, Ralph. 1952. *Invisible Man.* New York: Random House.

Giddens, Anthony, Mitchell Duneier, and Richard Applebaum. 2007. *Introduction to Sociology*, 6th ed. New York: McGraw-Hill.

Gladwell, Malcolm. 2002. *The Tipping Point: How Little Things Can Make a Big Difference*. New York: Little, Brown and Company.

Good Reads. 2014. Quotes by Gloria Steinem. Retrieved July 2013 (http://www.goodreads.com/author/quotes/57108.Gloria_Steinem).

Harrison, Nelson. 2012. Interview. "Psychologist says hip hop beats/ violent lyrics hypnotize kids and changes their behavior." Retrieved November 23, 2012 (http://www.techyville.com/2012/11/social-media/ psychologist-says-hip-hop-beatsviolent-lyrics-hypnotize-kids-and-changes-their-behavior/).

Hill Collins, Patricia. 2000. *Black Feminist Thought: Knowledge, Consciousness, and the Politics of Empowerment*, 2nd ed. New York: Routledge.

Howard, Daryl C. 1996. "Culturally-appropriate Strategies, Techniques, and Interventions for Counseling African American Males." M.Ed. Thesis, Department of Education and Counseling, University of Maryland Eastern Shore, Princess Anne, Maryland.

Ignorance. 2013. In *Merriam-Webster.com*. Retrieved August 18, 2013 (http://www.merriam-webster.com/dictionary).

Jackson, John. 2012. "The Urgency of Now." The Schott Foundation for Public Education. Retrieved July 2013 (http://blackboysreport.org/urgency-of-now.pdf).

Kunjufu, Jawanza. 1985. *Countering the Conspiracy to Destroy Black Boys*. Chicago, IL: African American Images.

Lauer, Robert H. and Jeanette C. Lauer. 2013. *Social Problems and the Quality of Life*, 13th ed. New York: McGraw-Hill.

Lee, Courtland C. 1992. *Empowering Young Black Males*. Ann Arbor, MI: ERIC Counseling and Personnel Services Clearinghouse.

Majors, R. and Nikelly, A. 1983. "Serving the Black Minority: A New Direction for Psychotherapy." *Journal of Non-White Concerns in Personnel and Guidance* 11:142-151.

McLeod, Saul. 2014. "Maslow's Hierarchy of Needs." Retrieved October 2014. (http://www.simplypsychology.org/maslow.html).

Obama, Barack. 2008. "A More Perfect Union" [Speech]. Presented at National Constitution Center, March 18, Philadelphia, PA.

Powell, Kevin. 2008. *Black Male Handbook*. New York: Atria Books.

Robinson, Eugene. 2010. *Disintegration: The Splintering of Black America*. New York: Doubleday.

Romney, Mitt. 2012. Speech. Presented at Otterbein University, April 27, Westerville, Ohio.

Ruiz, Rebecca. 2011. "A New Book Argues Against the SAT." New York Times, November 9. Retrieved November 9, 2011 (http://thechoice.blogs.nytimes.com/2011/11/09/sat/).

Russell, R.D. 1970. "Black Perceptions of Guidance." *Personal and Guidance Journal* 48:721-728.

Sandberg, Sheryl. 2013. *Lean In: Women, Work, and the Will to Lead.* New York: Alfred A. Knopf Publisher.

Schaefer, Richard T. 2010. *Sociology,* 12th ed. New York: McGraw-Hill Companies.

Shipp, P.L. 1983. "Counseling Blacks: A Group Approach." *The Personnel and Guidance Journal* 62:108-111.

Smith. Sandy. 2013. "Black Men: The Receptacle Into Which You Toss your Fears." Philly Mag, December 3. Retrieved December 3, 2013 (www.phillymag.com).

Sue, Derald W. 1981. *Counseling the Culturally Different: Theory and Practice.* New York: John Wiley and Sons.

The Glasser Insitute. 2013. Reality Therapy. Retrieved December 2013 (http://www.wglasser.com/the-glasser-approach/reality-therapy).

Tough, Paul. 2012. *How Children Succeed.* New York: Houghton Mifflin Harcourt.

Whitlock, Craig. 2008. "Racism Rears Its Head in European Remarks on Obama." *Washington Post,* November 11. Retrieved November 11, 2008 (www.washingtonpost.com).

Made in the USA
Middletown, DE
03 May 2021